THE GOSPEL AND THE PLOW

OR

THE OLD GOSPEL AND MODERN FARMING
IN ANCIENT INDIA

THE MACMILLAN COMPANY
NEW YORK · BOSTON · CHICAGO · DALLAS
ATLANTA · SAN FRANCISCO

MACMILLAN & CO., Limited
LONDON · BOMBAY · CALCUTTA
MELBOURNE

THE MACMILLAN CO. OF CANADA, Ltd.
TORONTO

THE
GOSPEL AND THE PLOW

OR

THE OLD GOSPEL AND MODERN FARMING
IN ANCIENT INDIA

BY

SAM HIGGINBOTTOM, M.A.

B.Sc. IN AGRICULTURE

New York
THE MACMILLAN COMPANY
1926

Copyright, 1921,
By THE MACMILLAN COMPANY

Set up and electrotyped. Published April, 1921

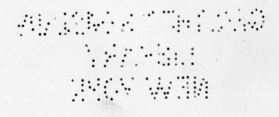

PRINTED IN THE U. S. A.

TO

THE ONE WITHOUT WHOSE UNFAILING COUR-
AGE, GOOD-TEMPER, FAITH IN GOD AND IN ME,
THIS BOOK COULD NEVER HAVE BEEN WRIT-
TEN; TO THE HELP-MEET AND PARTNER IN
ALL THE STRUGGLES REPRESENTED HEREIN

MY WIFE

PREFACE

This book is written at the request of the publishers who asked me to put into book form some lectures delivered at Princeton Theological Seminary. There is more in the book than the lectures. I feel that so little has been accomplished in India of all I set out to do, that this book is little more than a report of progress. There is a growing interest in the non-theological aspects of Foreign Missions and this production may serve some purpose in drawing attention to the need for other than the ordained missionary to help the backward peoples of the far countries. Those who are intimately acquainted with my work in India may feel that I have ignored altogether or slurred over some of the greatest difficulties to be faced in the establishment of such an institution as is contemplated at Allahabad.

It is said that I speak only of the high spots, tell only of the successes, write as though there were no humiliating failures to record. This is largely true. But any one familiar with the practical conduct of affairs knows that there are difficulties and lions in the way, that there is friction and clash of will, that there are sharp differences of opinion before any worthwhile program is carried out. So much so has this been my experience that I have come to see that the only place on earth where men are gathered together without friction is the cemetery. It is not altogether loss to be blind to some of the "insoluble problems." I have found that some of these with infinite patience, no bitterness of spirit or of jealousy, led by His spirit, can be made most useful. We are told that the mountains shall be a way, the seeming barriers shall be the paths to progress, so that I do not despair of seeing not only a new heaven, but also a new earth, wherein dwelleth righteousness. Therefore in hope and great expectancy I daily pray and work that His Kingdom may come here and now.

SAM HIGGINBOTTOM.

Radnor Road
Cleveland Heights, Ohio.
Dec. 27, 1920.

CONTENTS

"And thine ears shall hear a word behind thee saying, This is the way, walk ye in it, when ye turn to the right hand, and when ye turn to the left."   Isaiah 30 : 21.

"Neither are your ways my ways, saith the Lord. For as the heavens are higher than the earth, so are my ways higher than your ways."   Isaiah 55 : 8–9.

THE GOSPEL AND THE PLOW

CHAPTER I

In the month of February, 1903, while I was still an undergraduate in Princeton University, I was invited by an old school friend, Mr. W. W. Fry, then Secretary of the Trenton Y. M. C. A., to spend Sunday with him. I accepted his invitation, and accompanied him to the men's meeting on Sunday afternoon. When the meeting was over he introduced me to a missionary from India, the Rev. Henry Forman. On the following morning in the street car on which I rode back to College, the only vacant seat was beside the missionary to whom I had been introduced the day before, and whom I had never expected to see again. As soon as I had taken my seat he began to ask all manner of questions.

"What year are you in college?"

"This is my last," I answered.

"What next?"

"A theological seminary."

"Then what?"

"The foreign mission field, I hope."

"Where do you want to go?"

3

"Either to China or to South America."

"What do you think of India?"

"Not much."

"Why not?"

"Because the missionaries from India whom I have heard, all speak of the intellectual keenness and the nimble-mindedness of the Indian. I do not feel able to cope with that kind."

He then told me of the mass movement among the outcastes in which thousands of the lowest classes of India were turning to Christ. He suggested that, if I were willing and anxious for work, I should go out immediately after my course was finished at college to **work among these poor illiterate folk.** He also suggested that this would not be the kind of work which would overtax my mentality. In view of my age he thought that the Board might be willing to send me out. I could still take my theological course in India and be ordained later on. Then he put to me the direct question.

"If the Presbyterian Board would send you immediately upon graduation from college would you go out to India to do evangelistic work among the low-caste people?" I could, at the moment, think of no good reason against such a proposal, so, hesitatingly, replied that, although there was little hope of the Board sending me out as an unordained man for evangelistic work, yet I was ready to go.

"All right," he said. "Before you attend any lectures to-day write to Robert Speer and tell him of our conversation. I will also write. Good-by, I get off here." We had reached Lawrenceville which lies about half way between Trenton and Princeton. I had the rest of the journey in which to ride alone and think of what I had done. I prayed. When I reached my room, I wrote to Mr. Robert E. Speer. In April I was commissioned to go out unordained, to carry on evangelistic work among the low-caste people of North India. In New York City I was appointed to Etah, in the United Provinces of Agra and Oudh, India. I was graduated in June and started for India.

On Nov. 10, 1903, I arrived in Calcutta. I went northwest, five hundred and fourteen miles, to Allahabad, the nearest station at which the American Presbyterians were at work. After spending a few happy days as the guest of the late Dr. and Mrs. Arthur H. Ewing, I accompanied them to Ludhiana in the Punjab, where the Presbyterian synod was to meet. At the same time the Punjab and North India missions were to hold their annual meetings. Here I received a most cordial and hearty welcome from all the missionaries. I sat in the meetings and saw how the business of the mission was conducted. I noticed how much trouble was caused by the refusal of a certain missionary to accept the work which the missionary body assigned to him. I decided that I would never be so stubborn. I had little idea how soon and how keenly my decision would be put to the test. When the vacancies were considered, there were not nearly enough missionaries to go round. When my own turn came they surprised me by saying:— "We have decided that you are to teach in the college at Allahabad." I objected. "I had come out," I said, "to do evangelistic work. I did not like the idea of teaching, I was not fitted for it." It was pointed out that in the contract signed in New York I had agreed to abide by the will of a majority of the mission. The majority had voted that I was to go to the college at Allahabad. "All right," I said. "I am not willing to break my contract. I will do the best I can. I go under protest, and I do not hold myself responsible for results."

The more one studies the organization of a mission and the various ways and means which it employs in order to make Christ and His Good News known, the more one will find that it is the spirit and attitude of the individual missionary which matters rather than the particular work to which he is assigned. If one has the right attitude of mind and a broad and liberal education, then whatever the duty assigned, one will find a way of using his work to further the great end in view. For the individual who has once seen the vision of what the world might be if it had Jesus as Lord and Master, and who has consecrated himself to the will of God and to his fellow men in obedience to Jesus' "Go ye into all the world," it is not possible to conceive of any position in mission work in India which will not call out all the energy, power, initiative of which that individual is possessed. It is the fault of the missionary if he, or she, does not go tired to bed every night from a day well spent in the service of the Master. The mission merely assigns the new arrival to a station, it cannot give to him either the spirit or the personality with which to work out his faith. The individual has invariably to make his own way of presenting Christ. Whatever his appointment he has to determine for himself the best way of carrying his principles into practice. One of the joys of mission service is that the individual missionary has such a free hand, and is so much the master of his own work. During his first years he serves an apprenticeship in a very sympathetic company. The older missionaries are eager that the newcomer should find that work in which he can work with the least friction, and the work into which he can put all his heart and enthusiasm. The field is so great and the task is so complex and manysided that the missionary can use his own particular talent to gain other talents. No one method will meet all cases. Therefore each missionary, as he keeps in mind his purpose, can work out his life, according to his aptitudes and fitness, to hasten the coming of that Kingdom for which we daily pray.

The scarcity of missionaries was such that the Mission College at Allahabad was unable to ask what the teacher was best fitted to teach. It knew where its greatest need lay and simply told the teacher to fill it as best he could. The subjects upon which I was best prepared were already well cared for. I was assigned to a subject which I had taken at college simply for the reason that it was required.—They told me that I was to teach Economics.

The text books were English and American, the students were Indian and were forced to do their studying in a foreign language. Let an American undergraduate whose mother tongue is English, be required to do all his college work in a modern language, for example French, and he will then understand the hard task set the Indian student. Yet such is the curious situation in India that English is the language of the educated. It is the one language that will take one all over India. There is no one Indian language that will do this, although there are over one hundred different Indian languages spoken and written in India to-day. The English language, while having certain obvious disadvantages, has been a great blessing to India. From the English classics the Indian student has mastered some great world ideas that were dimly stated, or not stated at all, in oriental literature. These ideas are now bearing fruit. The great fact of the growth of a feeling of nationalism in India; the idea of democracy, the idea of human liberty, learned from Milton and the other English writers, are necessary antecedents of the idea of responsible government in India which will be a government in which the majority elected will be Indians. English has been a hard schoolmaster, but it has been a thorough one, and its teachings are now part of the warp and woof of the thinking of educated India. Nothing else could so surely and so quickly have made it possible for India to consider itself one people.

When these students found that their teacher knew so little about his subject, they were afraid that they would fail in their Government examinations. Up to this time the Indian University has been an examining body, not a teaching university, and no separate college can examine its own students or grant degrees. It was difficult to find Indian illustrations that the students could understand, for the various economic principles laid down in the text books. Granted the soundness of the principles, it was essential to obtain illustrations and concrete examples out of the Indian conditions which they knew. With this end in view we began to take advantage of the Indian holiday system, which perhaps needs a word of explanation. India possesses the largest Mohammedan population of any country in the world. It is greater than that of Egypt, Turkey, Persia, and Arabia put together and amounts to over seventy millions. When an Indian college admits Mohammedan students it is compelled to allow them to observe their own religious holidays and festivals. Again, India is the only country which has any very considerable Hindu population. At the last census this population numbered over two hundred and twenty millions, more in fact than the total of all the Protestant Christians in the world to-day. The Hindu students must also be free to observe their religious holidays. With the different Christian holidays added, including Sunday of course, the college term is somewhat broken up, and the Indian student, being in most things not unlike his fellow students the world over, takes full advantage of every holiday. I often recall a remark of President W. O. Thompson of Ohio State University, that education is the one commodity sold in America for which the purchaser is glad to receive less than he has paid for. The greater the number of holidays, the better the student likes it.

Realizing the difficulties which I have mentioned, of studying in a foreign language, and having an inexperienced teacher, the students agreed to give up some of these numerous holidays, in order that we might take trips together to study economic conditions in the neighborhood. Together we visited the workshops of the East India Railway and realized how human labor had been reduced to a minimum through the use of power, how the inventive genius of man is multiplying his own capacity and at the same time ridding human labor of its most forbidding drudgery. When they saw a pair of locomotive driving wheels on a lathe in a room where hardly a sound could be heard, they stood amazed at the exhibition of such tremendous power applied in quietness.   In the brick kilns we watched production on a large scale and the specialization of process.

We crossed the Jumna river in order to visit the Naini Central Jail which has accommodation for three thousand prisoners.   For sixteen years the Superintendant of this jail was the late Colonel E. Hudson, I.M.S., a British Military Medical officer.   Colonel Hudson was a genius.   He tried to manage the jail so that no man who entered should return to his ordinary life without having learned something which would be of advantage to him if he wished to become a decent citizen.   The gardens and the field crops were the best I have ever seen.   His field cabbages, crop after crop, weighed from forty to sixty pounds each.   His cauliflowers, stripped of all leaves and stalk, till only the beautiful snowy, white head remained, turned the scale at from fifteen to twenty pounds.   His silage crops of sorghum or millet grew to a height of from seventeen to eighteen feet, and weighed twenty-five to thirty tons of green fodder to the acre. Dean Alfred Vivian of the College of Agriculture, Ohio State University, Columbus, Ohio, on his journey round the world, rated the jail silage A No. 1.   Colonel Hudson invented a coal-burning stove for cooking the thin, flat, unleavened cakes of India, known as chappatties. This stove saved the jail twenty thousand rupees a year in fuel and the daily labor of fifty cooks.   In the days when the kitchens had been dependent upon wood for fuel, it had been almost impossible to obtain dry wood in the rainy season with which to cook the food.   As a result of damp wood and improperly cooked food, an outbreak of cholera and dysentery had accompanied the annual rainy season.   This coal stove alone had been the means of saving the lives of hundreds of prisoners.

There were machine shops, carpentering and woodcarving shops, and a pottery department; there were weaving sheds where the prisoners worked upon the most up-to-date hand-looms, making their own blankets and clothing; there was a rug factory, a roofing-tile factory and modern dairy which provided milk for the sick prisoners and jail staff. Various experiments had been carried on with underground silos and I have never seen cattle in better condition than those at the Naini jail fed on this silage. Colonel Hudson had learned how to appeal to the criminal mind and also how to get the best out of it. In every case he tried to send the man out a better man than when he came in. In his gardens and on his farm he had learned how best to turn the waste products from the jail into abundant health-producing food for man and beast. This was on land that had been considered sterile and unproductive when turned over to him. It did not take many visits to convince both the students and myself that if only Colonel Hudson's methods for the utilization of wastes could be copied all over India, more could be done with these than with any other single factor to rid India of the terrible famines which attack her periodically. The proper disposal of the refuse would give the people enough to eat and would provide a sanitary system which would greatly improve the general health. The organization of the jail was so nearly perfect, the efficiency so remarkable and the cleanliness so evident that the jail was a favorite visiting place for us and we never came away without feeling that the visit had been worth while. In Colonel Hudson we saw the type of public servant, quiet, alert, diligent, sympathetic, efficient, never looking for reward other than his regular pay, rejoicing in doing his duty

well, that has made Britain the most successful of the
colonizing nations of history.

"When thou goest out to battle against thine enemies, and seest horses, and chariots, and a people more than thou, be not afraid of them: for the Lord thy God is with thee, which brought thee up out of the land of Egypt. And it shall be, when ye are come nigh unto the battle, that the priest shall approach and speak unto the people, And shall say unto them, Hear, O Israel, ye approach this day unto battle against your enemies: let not your hearts faint, fear not, and do not tremble neither be ye terrified because of them; For the Lord your God is he that goeth with you, to fight for you against your enemies, to save you. And the officers shall speak unto the people, saying, What man is there that hath built a new house, and hath not dedicated it? let him go and return to his house, lest he die in the battle, and another man dedicate it. And what man is he that hath planted a vineyard, and hath not yet eaten of it? let him also go and return unto his house, lest he die in the battle, and another man eat of it. And what man is there that hath betrothed a wife, and hath not taken her? let him go and return unto his house, lest he die in the battle, and another man take her. And the officers shall speak further unto the people, and they shall say, What man is there that is fearful and fainthearted? let him go and return unto the house, lest his brethren's heart faint as well as his heart."   Deut. 20:1–8.

CHAPTER II

India is a land of villages, 700,000 of them. Her population is rural,—over ninety per cent. of the people living in small villages. We went into some neighboring villages in order to study the life of the Indian farmer. In the United Provinces the Indian farmer seldom has his home on his own farm land. The average holding of the tenant there is three and one half acres. The average farm of a land-owner is only four and one half acres. These small farms are usually scattered and "fragmented" into a number of small plots, very often distributed within a radius of a mile or so round the village. Because of these small scattered holdings the farmers usually live in the villages, securing protection against wild animals and wandering bands of criminals. The ordinary house has walls of solid mud, one story high and no cellar. The roof is a bamboo frame work over which is laid straw thatch or tiles about the size of a man's hand. The reason for the small sized tile is that it is hand molded and baked with cowdung for fuel which does not give enough heat to bake a large tile. There is generally not more than one room and one door. A verandah, six to ten feet wide, serves as shelter for the bullocks and the cow. Such a house costs from fifteen to fifty dollars to build. From our conversation with

13

these villagers we learned that they had little capital, very little equipment, and entirely insufficient food and clothing. Their capital generally consisted of:

One pair of work oxen, each...............$10.00 to $15.00
A wooden plow .... .65
A sickle for reaping grain...................... .30
A native spade for digging..................... .60
A grass cutting tool........................... .20
A wooden fork .... .20
A thick heavy club for breaking clods.............. .15
A flat board for leveling ground.................. .50
A few old Standard Oil tins...................... .50
A big leather bag, maintenance per year ....
A long rope 6.00
A pulley wheel 1.00

$25.10

This list usually represents the number of their agricultural implements. The plow is a wooden one with a small iron tip or bar, keel shaped like a boat. It does not turn a furrow, but makes a small V shaped scratch throwing the dirt on each side. This scratch is so narrow that to plow an acre means going over the ground at least three times; the distance walked is over fifty miles. A small, improved plow that turns a furrow will do a better job and go only sixteen miles to plow the acre. The ordinary Indian plow has only one handle so the plowman is near enough to twist the tails of his oxen. Seeing this plow one understands why Jesus said, '' No man, having put his hand to the plow, and looking back is fit for the Kingdom of God.'' If the Indian plowman looks back the plow will not stay in the furrow, but rides out, and fails to accomplish the purpose for which it was made. And that is the point of Jesus' remark. The man who looks back fails to accomplish what he

should.   The Indian spade or "pharwa" is shaped like
a large hoe with a short handle.   It takes less muscular
effort and accomplishes less work than an American
spade or shovel.   But when we see how hard Indian soil
can bake and consider the fact that so few Indian farmers wear shoes, we realize that the Indian type is better
suited to Indian conditions for digging than the American.   When it comes to shovelling sand, lime, coal or
dirt it is not nearly so efficient as the American type.
Wherever an American shovel is used in India it is a
two-man job; one man pushes and steers the shovel, another has a rope attached at the lower end of the handle
and pulls on it.

The grass cutting tool is generally a bit of old buggy
tire sharpened at one end and bent at the other end for
a handle.   When grass is to be cut the man takes hold
of a handful of grass in the left hand and pushes the
cutting tool a little under the surface of the ground to
get all he can, root and all, so that a freshly cut hay
field has no stubble in sight, but looks as though it had
been harrowed.   The method of cutting grass in India
is an interesting side light on the cheapness of human
life and the expensiveness of grass.

The Standard Oil tin occupies an unique place in the
domestic economy of India.   It used to be very cheap,
about five cents a tin.   It is now worth thirty.   It is
used for storing seed, jewelry, oil, water, in fact anything that needs a water-tight container that can resist
white ants.   When worn out the sides are used for roof-
ing houses and temples.

Comparing the Indian farmer's capital invested in his
land with the investment of the average American farmer
the total is very small, and the investment per acre is

almost negligible in India as compared with the improved farm lands in America. The family of the Indian tenant farmer usually plans for one meal a day. During part of the year this meal is often uncooked and consists of millet soaked in cold water, or a pulse parched in hot sand and eaten a grain at a time. When pulse is cooked, it forms pigeon pea-soup, which is seasoned with spices, red peppers or chilis. Into this soup are dipped the cakes of unleavened bread which have been cooked over a small fire of dried cowdung. This unleavened bread usually is made from the cheaper grains, since wheat is, as a rule, too expensive for these poor villagers. The strict upper-caste Hindu is a vegetarian, but the low-caste man with whom Hinduism is little more than a thin veneer, will eat any meat, except that of the cow or ox. Under the influence of caste the outcastes have organized themselves into castes with all the limitations thereof. One of these low-castes will eat the flesh of the cow, provided they have not killed it. Once the animal is dead they ask no questions as to the manner of its death, whether from disease or old age, but cook it and eat it. Sometimes they do not cook it.

I remember a little girl of about fourteen who was working on the Mission farm clearing out the cowstables, earning four cents a day. We have no difficulty in getting all the labor we need because we pay more than the market rates, work is regular, full pay is there on pay day without fines or deductions.

This girl was married and rejoicing in her first baby boy. I noticed that after the work oxen had gone out to plow this little Indian mother would lay her dear little brown baby son in the manger, just as once another Little Baby was laid in a manger. She would fill her basket with cowdung, put the basket on her head, carry it out to the fields where it was to do its work, then return for another load, and each time she came back she loved and fondled her little one. She was a glad, happy, proud little mother, singing at her work. The Maharajah of Bikaner, that Indian King who was one of the Indian representatives at the Peace Conference in Paris, invited me to draw up a scheme for agricultural development in his country. It involved travel over the state and took me about three weeks. When I returned to Allahabad the little mother was walking round sad and disconsolate. I said "Hello Nanki, what is the matter?" "O Sahib, he died," she replied. "Why did you not take him to the Mem-Sahib. You know my wife would have given you medicine for him?" She answered, "It was not medicine he needed but food. I could not nurse him. With four cents a day, could I buy milk for him and food for myself? Why Sahib, if I could not nurse him he had to die." Many Indian mothers have Nanki's experience.

Investigators like Sir William Hunter or Lord Curzon, or those Indian gentlemen who have spoken of the poverty of their country in the Indian National Congress, whether pro- or anti-British, are all agreed that the average per capita income for India ranges between seven and twenty-five dollars per year. This works out at less than three to six cents per day per person for the whole population. When we remember that India has a large and wealthy class of lawyers, merchants, money-lenders and landlords, it is obvious that many of the village folk have less than three cents a day upon which to live. About one third of the people of India are living at a rate of about two cents per day or less, are permanently underfed and ill-nourished, are so short of food that they do not get proper growth and are generally too weak to do a fair day's work.

Now a cent does not buy more of the necessities of life in India than it does in America, for the price for grain is fixed by world conditions; wheat is in a world market. Cotton cloth made in Lancashire from American cotton, competes with cloth made from cotton grown, spun and woven in India.

It simply means that Indians, in number approximating the population of the United States, about one hundred million, have not yet come to regard as possible luxuries many things which America's poorest regard as absolute necessities. No one can understand India who ignores this degrading, debasing poverty which is one inseparable link in the vicious circle of ignorance, superstition, oppression, ill-health, infant mortality, lack of sanitation and the continued persistence of such epidemic diseases as cholera, dysentery, plague, enteric, malaria, hook-worm, small-pox and other preventable ills. It is a poverty which robs manhood, womanhood, and childhood of all that is best and most worthwhile in them. India's poverty is a menace to the rest of the world. A prosperous India producing more of the things she can most easily produce could exchange them for the manufactured articles she needs but cannot produce. Self-interest, as well as sympathy, demands that a remedy be found for India's poverty.

In many villages with from one hundred to three hundred inhabitants, one could not find one person, man or woman, who could read or write. Sir Michael E. Sadler, K.C.S.I., in reviewing "Village Education in India," shows that half a million of villages in British India are unsupplied by a primary school. (International Review of Missions—October 1920.) The last census taken ten years ago gives the degree of literacy as five and six tenths per cent. where the test was the ability to write a letter of four to five simple sentences in any one of the languages of India, and to read the reply to it. This shows that about ten per cent. of the men and boys are literate, and about one per cent. of the women and girls over ten years of age. Now when any people is so largely illiterate it is an easy prey for oppression and extortion. Wild rumors find ready credence. A lie once started is not easily caught up and corrected. India suffers in full measure the penalty for so great a degree of ignorance. Illiteracy immensely increases the troubles of government, especially when the government is a foreign one. A demagogue determined to make trouble can go among an illiterate people and stir them up into a state of frenzy by telling either deliberate falsehoods, or by so twisting the truth as to misrepresent it. It is very difficult for the Government to correct this, since the harm is done before the Government is aware of it. At the root of hatred, is fear, and at the root of fear, is ignorance. Once the hatred and suspicion have been aroused, it requires months of hard work to put out the flame, and to establish peace. Any one who is familiar with modern India and who is watching with deepest sympathy and good will the progress of the greatest adventure in democratic government which the world has ever seen, cannot but wonder at its chances of success when ninety four and four-tenths per cent. of the population is illiterate. The educated Indian is the peer of any educated man anywhere, and as fit for self-government.

Six millions have been enfranchised in India. The leadership rests on about a quarter of a million who have the necessary education. It is the uneducated Indians that constitute the problem. I am anxious to see the day when India shall take her proper place as one of the great self-governing peoples of the world. The British officials and the European commercial community have put on record their desire actively to assist in making the Montague Chelmsford Reforms a success, but many more schools will have to be built and filled with Indian boys and girls before India will be able to accept her fair share of the responsibilities of the world, and carry her part of the burden of modern civilization.

Bad and crippling as this lack of education is among the men of India, in order to see the most far-reaching and cumulative evil effects of illiteracy it is necessary to realize the meaning of illiteracy among the women and girls of India. When we consider the inferior social status of women in India; the purdah system which shuts them off by themselves, keeps them prisoners for life, often in insanitary, ill-lighted, ill-ventilated quarters; the fact that women are by nature more conservative than men; and that in the early and most impressionable days of life the children are under the care of mothers, only one out of a hundred of whom can write her own name; we ask what chance has the Indian boy or girl compared with the American boy or girl? The illiterate Indian mother has her mind filled with superstition, myth, suspicion, and the consequent dread and terror and darkness that cramp and dwarf life. The mother can convey to her child only what she herself has in her own mind. The woman of India has had it impressed upon her that she is inferior to the man. She is often a chattel, degraded, debased. This treatment causes her to lose her self-respect. A survey of the field of Indian life shows no more devitalizing handicap clamped upon a great people than the illiteracy of the nation's motherhood. There is most urgent need that the Christian women of the world help their illiterate sisters in India to receive the same generous heritage which they themselves take as a matter of course, seldom realizing that they owe their position of equality with men, and freedom to decide their own life's partner and work, to Jesus, who is the world's first Gentleman. It is only as Christian men obey Him that woman has a chance as an individual with a soul, and a right to choose her own life, to control her own person, and to say who shall be the father of her children.

The causes for India's poverty are many, but the chief of them are such as can only be removed by the Indians themselves for they are related to the religion of the Hindus. I believe the causes for India's poverty to be: 1. Caste; 2. Too many cattle that are an economic loss to the country; 3. The great army of able-bodied men, over five millions of them, who toil not neither do they spin, the religious mendicants or "faqirs." But the greatest of these is Caste.

"And it shall come to pass, if ye shall hearken diligently unto my commandments which I command you this day, to love the Lord your God, and to serve him with all your heart and with all your soul, That I will give you the rain of your land in his due season, the first rain and the latter rain, that thou mayest gather in thy corn, and thy wine, and thine oil. And I will send grass in thy fields for thy cattle, that thou mayest eat and be full. Take heed to yourselves that your heart be not deceived, and ye turn aside and serve other gods and worship them. And then the Lord's wrath be kindled against you, and he shut up the heaven, that there be no rain, and that the land yield not her fruit; and lest ye perish quickly from off the good land which the Lord giveth you." Deut. 11 : 13–17.

"Neither is there salvation in any other: for there is none other name under heaven given among men, whereby we must be saved." Acts 4 : 12.

CHAPTER III

CASTE, A LIMITING FACTOR

Observation shows that the "Caste System," that bed-rock of the Hindu religion, is the fundamental cause for India's poverty, in that it is the greatest factor in limiting production. It does this in a number of ways. For instance—I employed a sweeper whose work kept him occupied for less than two hours a day. His wages were two dollars a month. Indian servants feed themselves. He had a wife and six children. When I paid him his wages he held it in his hand and looked at it. He said, "Sahib, it is very hard to feed eight people on such a small sum." I answered that I did not see how he did it. I said, "I would like to pay you more money if you earned it. The gardener has asked for help to dig in the garden. If you will go and help him I will gladly pay you." He replied that he would go and dig in the garden. He started in to work. In a few minutes the gardener came to me and asked for his pay. I said, "What is the matter? Are you not satisfied with your work? Do I not treat you fairly?" He replied, "O yes, Sahib, you treat me all right and the work is all right, but I must leave." "Why? What is the matter that you cannot work?" "Well, Sahib, you have sent that sweeper to work in the garden. If he stays I go." "But, you asked me for aid and I sent him to help you. He has a wife and six children and gets two dollars a

23

month. You have a wife and four children and get two and a half dollars a month. Yet, you complain of the difficulty. How much harder then for him. So I thought if he were willing to work extra, I would pay him for it, and you would get your digging done and he would have more food for his family." "Yes, Sahib that is all true, but you see he is not of my caste and so cannot work in the garden with me. If he stays, I go. If I stay while he works in the garden my castefellows will not drink water or smoke the huqqa with me, and I cannot suffer the disgrace of this just for a sweeper. So I must leave." I call the sweeper away from the garden and explain the trouble to him. He understands perfectly well the reason. We both know that if the gardener leaves, I cannot get another. They would boycott me if I allowed my gardener to leave for such a reason. So the sweeper must look otherwhere to sell his labor, and always with the same result, so with sad, resigned air he accepts his fate. Not the oppression of the Indian by the foreigner, but the oppression of the Indian by the system of caste which is the heart and essence of the religion of the Hindus. Certain castes may not touch the plow or the digging tool; others may not apply manure to their fields. Caste is often behind the prejudice against the introduction of labor saving machinery. Certain castes may grow field crops but may not grow vegetables, others may grow vegetables but not field crops. In America it is the custom for nearly every farmer to have a garden in which is grown, in season, sufficient fresh vegetables for the family. The discovery of the importance of the "vitamines" which exist in fresh, green vegetables and in milk and fruit and the part which they play in the growth and development of human beings, indicates that not a little of the malnutrition of India is due to the absence of fresh vegetables in the diet of the farmer. This limiting of production is one of the economic aspects of caste, but the caste system also has its religious and its social aspects.

"In Southern India, as is well known, there exist immense numbers of so-called untouchable classes, to whom, particularly on the Malabar side, are denied what might be called the elementary rights of human beings. They are condemned to live far beyond the outskirts of the villages; they are forbidden to use many of the public roads; their very approach within a certain number of yards is accounted contamination. As a result of this, these depressed classes live in hovels and seem to delight in dirt. From a casual appearance it would appear that the great majority of them have lost whatever innate love of cleanliness human beings may be expected to possess. They have no education, because they cannot afford to take advantage of it even if it is proffered free. They have no outlook in life; they are condemned to the most degrading forms of labor. But the root of the matter is less economic than social. Until these depressed classes can be put on a level with their fellow-men, can be treated as equals, and relieved from the moral degradation into which they have been thrown by centuries of scorn, it is difficult to do very much with them. Official orders can be passed in such directions as insisting that children of the depressed classes should be admitted into schools, that members of these classes should have proper houses and free access to the public water-supply; but in the absence of public opinion it is quite impossible for Government to enforce these orders which fly in the face of habits centuries old. In addition to the particular problems presented by the untouchable class, which are principally characteristic of Southern India, there is also the All-India problem of the general condition of the peasantry. Recent settlement operations in certain parts of Northern India have revealed that in some places, the average agricultural laborer is not infrequently compelled in time of stress to mortgage his personal liberty. In return for a small sum of money, which he may happen to need at the moment, he agrees to serve the man from whom he has borrowed. The money is not repaid, nor is it intended to be repaid; but the borrower remains the life-long bond slave of his creditor. For his work he merely receives an inadequate dole of food, and to all intents and purposes is in the position of a mediæval serf." (From "India in 1919," pp. 125–126.)

In its religious aspect caste fixes the status of the individual by birth, and birth alone. It determines what a man shall do and the manner of his doing it for the whole of his existence on this earth. By identifying conduct with religion many things which are not desirable from the standpoint of sanitation and health are indissolubly linked through caste with the Hindu religion. These may not be interfered with by the British government, which has held the good-will of India in the past, largely because it has been neutral in religion, and has made it its policy to interfere in matters religious as little as possible. It is true that Government interfered with the custom "Suttee" whereby the widow was burnt alive upon the funeral pyre of her dead husband, but it did not gain any popular credit for this interference. The widow was and still is regarded as the actual cause of her husband's death, and possessed of an evil spirit.

Therefore the widow is a "kill-joy" in any family, a person who would bring bad luck to any festive gathering. For this reason it was regarded as better that she with her evil spirit, should depart with her dead husband even though that meant burning alive. Again it is very difficult to-day for a Hindu woman to obtain proper attention at child-birth. At this time she is considered ceremonially unclean, and so can be attended only by low-caste midwives who display an amazing unwillingness to adopt either cleanly habits or modern ideas. Perhaps it would be fairer to say that their ideas of cleanliness are different from our own, for the newly born babe is usually treated with a dust bath or mud plaster which frequently causes lock-jaw, for the soil of India is impregnated with tetanus germs.

From another aspect caste is the direct denial of human brotherhood as understood in the New Testament. Caste separates men into water-tight compartments, caste insists that men born of woman differ in kind. Some at the top of the scale are "twice born" or "divine," others at the bottom of the scale are inferior or in the significant phraseology of their own countrymen called "untouchable" and considered sub-human. It is impossible for caste adherents to pray *"Our* Father" and yet these two words applied to God in the Lord's prayer contain the idea upon which all human brotherhood, and therefore all human justice, is founded. A low caste Hindu who had been trained in Western medicine, a highly educated gentleman, was haled into court at Calicut for polluting a village tank because he, a low-caste man, walked within a certain distance of the tank. He was acquitted, but the case caused much excitement. (See p. 129, "India in 1919.")

To return to what is both the social and economic
aspect of caste. There is an unwillingness to have sanitary latrines in the villages. The people go out into the
fields to relieve themselves and fail completely to follow
the Mosaic law in this matter (Deut. 23:13) of the disposing of refuse. Such an omission is the inevitable
cause of widespread disease, the contamination of the
water supply, and the fouling of all approaches to the
village. Added to objections of this nature, caste re-
stricts marriage within very narrow limits, caste prevents those social amenities which the Westerner as-
sociates with his meal times and therefore hinders the
consequent interchange of ideas. It supports a joint
family system in which all share alike, where the drones
and the ne'er-do-wells can take the heart out of the working members of the family by refusing to work, but in-
sist upon being fed. It causes the minute distribution
of all property and thus lies behind the present un-
economic system of land holding where the farm is broken
up into scattered strips and into holdings so small as to
prevent a family from obtaining a decent living from the
produce of such a tiny acreage.

Let it be understood, however, that in this criticism
of the system of caste as it stands to-day, condemnation
is not wholesale. Caste is not all bad. It has its good
side. Surely a system which has succeeded in holding
a great people together for untold centuries must have
in it elements of unusual cohesive strength. The trouble
is that caste has undergone so little change that it has
failed to adapt itself to the changing conditions of human life. Caste is outgrown. It is an anachronism in
a world in which the railroad, the telegraph, the penny

post, the steam-boat and the printing press have ceased to be seven day wonders.

There are over fifty millions of outcastes or "untouchables" in India. Men and women at the bottom of the social scale, who do the lowest and meanest tasks, some are scavengers, some will eat carrion, some are filthy and disgusting in their habits. They have been kept down by the higher castes. They have been denied the right to education, to worship in the temples, to own or read the sacred scriptures of the Hindus. They are said to be born at the bottom of a horrible pit and born to stay there. They are considered to be in their proper place, and there is no way out. They are considered to be in the place assigned them by the Almighty and under orthodox Hinduism there is no possibility for them to rise. **They are degraded and debased, kept down by** unmeasured centuries of oppression and tyranny.

The missionaries of Christ have gone among these lowly, despised folk and have told them of the One who came to heal the broken hearted, to deliver the captive, to set at liberty them that are bruised. This message is so different from anything else that they have ever heard that it seems almost too good to be true. It is hard to persuade them that there is a way out of their unspeakable degradation and bondage and poverty. But some of them are persuaded and are coming out. They are turning their faces towards the light and following it. Over fifteen thousand a month are becoming Christian and it is this Christward tide of humanity that has been called the "Mass Movement in India." Whole villages of certain low-castes are being baptized at one time. If only one or two come out at one time, they are so persecuted that missions hesitate to accept them. It is better to wait till the few have gained more. The whole village is better able to protect itself in its new faith than the isolated individual. Many more than actually are baptized each month want to be baptized, but because of lack of missionaries and lack of properly trained Indian preachers and teachers, the Christians of India are saying to the greatest Godward tide of history "Not quite so fast, you are swamping us, we cannot take care of you, wait till we get caught up with our schools and teachers and churches and preachers." The problems of Christian missions in India to-day are not problems caused by failure to get converts but are problems caused by the successes of so great an ingathering that we have not room to contain so great a harvest. The percentage of illiteracy is growing in the Christian church in India to-day. Only seventeen per cent. of the Christians can read or write. It is not because the missions are doing less educational work. They are actually doing more. The low-caste converts are almost totally illiterate and it is this great illiterate host of believers that are increasing the percentage of illiteracy.

There was a day when the missionary felt that baptism was the end. To-day he knows it is only the beginning. When these people come they are still poor, still ignorant, their eyes not yet clear, so that they see men as trees, walking. They have in them the inheritance of centuries of oppression and degradation. If we only baptize them and leave them alone we do them infinite harm. Baptized they are babes in Christ and need the milk of the Word that they may grow up to the full measure of the stature of men in Christ Jesus. How can we help such a lowly, dependent folk, who have no traditions of independence or liberty to brace them? If we dole out charity to them we rob them of the very thing they need training in most of all. It is not doles of charity they need but help to help themselves. Teach them by their own efforts how to earn their own living, and such a living as will enable them not only to have enough to eat, and to be decently clothed, but a living which contemplates education for the children, contributions to schools and churches, to hospitals and libraries, a living which enables them to take full responsibility as citizens.

I believe the best and quickest way to do this is to train them in agriculture, train the best and brightest in a good central institution so that the ones so trained can go out to their own folk in the villages. The ones trained in modern farming can earn much more than the untrained, so much more in fact that they can pay their own way and take their part as self-supporting members of the community. Some people who have seen this mass movement work criticize it. They say these people do not understand Christianity, that their motives are mixed and often unworthy, that they come to Christ for what they can get out of Him, that they are mercenary Christians, that they come for the loaves and fishes, that they are rice Christians. Having said so much they think the work is condemned and the case closed, but is it? Grant all they say, it means that these poor folk see in Christianity more than in their old faith. While adhering to their old faith material progress was impossible, under Christianity it is possible. Under their old faith they were denied common human rights, under Christianity they are recognized as brothers, under their old faith they were denied the spiritual resources of that faith, under Christianity their only limit is their capacity to comprehend the length and breadth and depth and height of the love of God for the lost. It always seems to me that Jesus must have had the low-caste in mind when He stated His mission to be to seek and to save that which was lost. After all, it is not the motive with which men or women come to Christ that matters, but the motive with which they stay with Him, and many can bear witness that God is raising up to Himself out of these whom man despises, a body of believers that are the spiritual equals of any body of believers anywhere on earth. In faithfulness even to death, in the last great supreme sacrifice for His dear sake, they are abundant witnesses. The low-caste converts educated in our mission schools and colleges often attain positions of distinction and high responsibility. They move freely among high-caste people, where, had they not been converted and trained, they never could have gone. As I see the progress of these masses to Jesus I come to see that the only cure for caste is Christ. That He effectually takes away any disability that caste causes. That in this life if any man be in Christ Jesus he is a new creation.

"And Moses said unto the children of Israel, See, the Lord hath called by name Bezaleel the son of Uri, the son of Hur, of the tribe of Judah; And he hath filled him with the spirit of God, in wisdom, in understanding, and in knowledge, and in all manner of workmanship; And to devise curious works, to work in gold, and in silver, and in brass, And in the cutting of stones, to set them, and in carving of wood, to make any manner of cunning work. And he hath put in his heart that he may teach, both he, and Aholiab, the son of Ahisamach, of the tribe of Dan. Them hath he filled with wisdom of heart, to work all manner of work, of the engraver, and of the cunning workman, and of the embroiderer, in blue, and in purple, in scarlet, and in fine linen, and of the weaver, even of them that do any work, and of those that devise cunning work."　　　　　　　Exodus 35: 30–35.

CHAPTER IV

MISSION INDUSTRIES

As I had gone to India to work among the outcaste people I was eager to see what the work was like, so on some of the longer college vacations I went to Etah where I had originally hoped to go to work among the outcastes. I also went on tour with Mr. and Mrs. Bandy and saw the thousands of converts gathered in by this devoted, original and energetic couple. I saw the great poverty of these new converts, I watched them bring in their gifts of eggs, chickens, grain and potatoes as well as of cash. I found that most of them were tithing, that is, were giving one-tenth of all they received of money or produce in order to support their preachers and teachers and to build their churches and schools. I also saw that where the family income, whether measured in money or in kind, was two dollars a month it was impossible for a tenth of so small a sum to do all that was needed to bring about a self-supporting church. I looked forward and tried to imagine the day when the missionary program in India should have been completed. A self-supporting, self-governing, self-propagating Christian church seemed the minimum for which to look forward. It was obvious that if the average church member was living at a rate of from one to three cents per person per day something would have to be done to increase the earning capacity and the income of the

34

church membership.   What looked like a purely ecclesias-
tical problem had an economic aspect that could not
be ignored.

I noticed that most of the large mission stations had
some kind of industrial work.   Iron-working, carpentry,
shoe-making and tailoring were the favorite occupations.   The great famines had left thousands of orphan
children to be cared for.   America was keeping many of
these thousands alive by subscribing at the rate of fifteen
dollars per orphan per year to feed, clothe and train
these boys and girls.   But fifteen dollars was not enough
to do this properly for a year.   Although so little was
spent upon the children, the Missions expected a return
in the improvement of the children similar to what an
American child in the public school system would show.
Great dissatisfaction was expressed that the children
developed so slowly and when turned out of the orphanage were able to earn so little.   How much could
American children have done under the same kind of
treatment?   Investigation shows that education is an
investment which in general pays the largest cumulative
dividend on the largest investment.   Not enough was invested in the low-caste convert or in the famine orphan
to earn a satisfactory dividend.   Some of the missionaries were actually afraid of doing humanitarian work
or of being interested in social service.   The division
was made between "real mission work" and educational and industrial work done by missionaries.   The
immortal soul, they said, was bound for eternity and
must therefore receive the chief emphasis.   The saving
of the soul was the chief end of the missionary effort,
and the less the missionary had to do with the body and
the material things which the body demanded in order

to be strong, healthy and efficient, the better for him. They used to talk of the great danger of the "rice converts," of those who followed for the loaves and fishes and of those who sought material gain. The Bible says, "What? know ye not that your body is the temple of the Holy Ghost . . . therefore glorify God in your body." Cor. 6:19-20. The body surely has its rightful demand for care and protection.

Investigation shows that most mission industrial enterprises in orphanages and for low-caste converts are failures, that generally, just as soon as a mission could close down its industrial work it did so, and only opened again when famine provided large numbers of children to be cared for. The causes of failure are:

First: The lack of properly and technically trained missionaries. Seldom did a mission have a member, man or woman, with the necessary technical training to make industrial work a success. Most missionaries have special training for evangelistic work, that does not imply the training necessary for a good blacksmith, or carpenter or shoe-maker. It would be much wiser for Foreign Mission Boards to take a leaf out of business experience and to appoint missionaries who have had special training for the particular piece of work to be done. An evangelist for evangelistic work: a blacksmith for iron work: a carpenter for working in wood: a farmer for farming. All should be controlled by that One Spirit without which no mission work can succeed. "There are diversities of operations, but it is the same God which worketh all in all."

Granted that a certain ordained evangelist who had been brought up on a farm, and remembers the labors of his youth makes a success of managing an orphanage, making up in enthusiasm what he lacks in technical skill, the boys under such a missionary may be passably trained in their particular trade, so that, if the missionary does the business managing and the marketing, they are able to earn anywhere from three to ten dollars per month.

Perhaps this successful missionary goes on furlough or dies. The mission has to make provision for his work. Often the most awkward, three-cornered person, who cannot fit in anywhere else, and who ought to be sent home, is put in charge of the industrial work because it is argued that he will do less harm to "real mission work" there than anywhere else. Some of the mission industries are big enough and involve sums of money large enough to demand real business management. The mission usually makes no provision for the continuity of the industrial work; when one man drops out there is no specially trained man to step in. If missions are going to engage in industry at all, it would be well to see that properly trained men and sufficient capital are obtained in order to carry it on with some measure of success. I take it that in a country like India, with famine ever threatening and poverty ever present, missions will be compelled to continue in industrial work for some time to come.

Second: The reason for failure often is:—the industry chosen is not suitable, or located in the wrong place with respect to markets. The caste system, in its economic aspect gives to each separate trade or occupation a far greater power and control over its members than a trades union claims over its members in America. If the missionary trains a boy for one of these caste trades he has to employ the boy whom he has trained.

If the boy leaves the mission in order to follow his trade in the open market he immediately comes into conflict with the caste trades union which will not only not admit him, but which will boycott anyone who employs him, until he is compelled to fall back into the ranks of the casual laborer and thus the missionaries' effort is largely wasted. The boy also does not get a fair chance in life.

Then too it is not worth while for a missionary to devote his life to teaching shoe-making, tailoring, carpentering or blacksmithing in India. When a Christian boy is trained to any of these trades, even if there were not the difficulty of caste tradesmen to contend with, the wages he can earn at present are not such that he can live decently and bring up a family on them. His prewar wages in Northern India would have been about sixteen cents per day. Wages have risen but so have prices. It is essential for missions to train their converts in those callings where they are not likely to run counter to any caste trades union and where they may be sure of earning a living wage. There are less caste restrictions in farming than in any other occupation, and those restrictions that do exist, usually apply to the higher, rather than to the lower castes.

India is about one million eight hundred thousand square miles in extent, that is, one-half the size of the United States and Alaska. Nearly one million square miles is culturable. About two hundred and fifty thousand square miles are forest. The rest is called unculturable waste. Much of this unculturable waste can be reclaimed by modern methods of drainage; by prevention of erosion; by washing out harmful salts from alkali lands; and by use of power plowing machinery.

According to the official report prepared for presentation in Parliament—"India in 1919"—India has eighty million acres in rice, and grows the largest amount of rice of any country in the world.

India in the season of 1919–1920 had about thirty million acres sown to wheat and grew over ten million tons of that staple, which was three million tons more than the year before.

India had the largest acreage under sugar cane (about half the world's area under sugar cane is in India) and until 1918 grew more cane sugar than any other country on earth. The yield of sugar for 1918 was estimated at three million seven hundred thousand tons.

India grows and exports more tea than any other country in the world, three hundred and eighty million pounds in 1918.

India leads the world in the production of oil seeds; castor, linseed, mustard, sesamum, cocoa-nut and peanut oils.

India leads the world in the production of sorghums and millets; pigeon pea and other edible legumes. India grows about eighty million tons of food grains a year.

India has a world monopoly in the growing of jute, from which all our gunny bags and sacks are made.

India leads the world in the production of shellac for varnish.

In 1919 India grew six million eight hundred thousand bales of cotton on over twenty million acres, each bale weighing four hundred pounds.

India has several million acres under "Sanai" which yields a fiber like hemp.

India has two hundred and sixty million head of horned cattle and water buffaloes.

India is rich in fruits which include, on the plains, the mango, the banana, the papita, the custard apple, the bear jack fruit, the orange and citrous fruits, in the mountains grow apples, pears, cherries, peaches, plums, apricots and strawberries. Many of these were introduced by Dr. Carleton of the American Presbyterian Mission.

The largest silk mill in the world is in Kashmir.

India is rich in spices and condiments of all kinds.

India mined over twenty-one million tons of coal during the last year for which figures were published. Oil has just been found in India proper.

This list is not exhaustive. It shows the large aggregate production in India of the world's staple crops and their wide variety. On the investigation of details it is found that India in general uses to-day the same tools and implements that she used in the time of Moses, that the yields of these crops per acre of land, or per man engaged on the land raising the crop, are the lowest for any civilized country on earth, this in spite of the fact that India's soil is naturally fertile, and the growing season so long.

The British Government started an Agricultural Department nearly thirty years ago. The staff of scientists has been somewhat small but the results amazing. Mr. and Mrs. Howard, Imperial Economic Botanists, bred ''The Pusa Series'' of wheat which was sown on over half a million acres last year. It is only ten years since this breed of wheat was in the experimental plot stage. The net increase due to this good seed is at least five dollars per acre per year better than the local varieties it displaced, with the present methods and implements. But this improved seed responds to better methods in a way the local varieties do not, so that when the better methods are introduced a net increase is obtained of fifty to one hundred per cent. more than the local varieties yield. Dr. Barber, Imperial Botanist, worked on sugar cane for seven years. The local variety of cane sugar grown in Northern India is a thin, hard cane chosen because of its power to resist the attacks of the wild pig, jackal, deer and disease. It responds only slightly to manuring and better cultivation. It gives about ten tons of cane per acre and less than a ton of sugar. The improved variety of cane is giving up to forty tons of cane per acre with over four tons of sugar.

Most of India's cotton is short staple, coarse fiber, low-yielding, ginning percentage 25-33 (the ginning percentage is the proportion of fiber or lint to seed). Most of the Indian varieties have a hairy leaf. Most good long staple cottons have a smooth leaf. The smooth leaf is readily attacked by insects while the hairy leaf is not. Mr. Leake, Director of Agriculture of the United Provinces at Cawnpur, has crossed different varieties of cotton so that he now has a hairy-leafed, long-staple cotton with a high-ginning percentage of 35–40 per cent. This cotton is worth more per pound than the short staple. Mr. Roberts, Principal of the Agricultural College at Lyalpur, Punjab, has done much to increase the yields and quality of American cotton grown in the Punjab. He has further devised a scheme for selling this improved cotton which gives a fair share of the increase to the farmer who grew the cotton.

Mr. Clouston, Director of Agriculture for the Central Provinces, has isolated a high yielding local variety, "Roseum," which gives five dollars an acre net profit more than the local variety. A breed of rice has been isolated for Bengal which gives twenty per cent. more than the local varieties. Plant diseases have been studied and in some cases remedies found. New varieties have been introduced. Coöperative credit societies for purchasing and marketing have been organized. Twenty-nine thousand societies are now active. When we recall that modern agricultural science is so recent in America, what India has done compares very favorably with what other countries have done, after due allowance has been made for all the unusual difficulties of the situation. If there is any place for criticism of the Government it is in the fact that methods were not devised and staff not provided for the spreading among the Indian farmers of the results of laboratory and experimental research. Efforts to this end are now being put forth but the area is so vast, it takes so long for a foreigner trained in agriculture to get acquainted with the Indian conditions; the ignorance, the suspicion, the illiteracy and superstition of the Indian farmers so widespread, that progress is necessarily slow. The illiterate Indian farmer has for centuries been fair game for anyone to exploit. It is difficult for him to believe that anyone is really trying to help him. When any improvement is being introduced he always imagines that some new trick is being played upon him. The Government is establishing rural, middle and high agricultural schools but is compelled to go slowly because of the dearth of properly qualified teachers with the right attitude towards the villager. It is at this particular point that America can be of the greatest service to India. America in the South, among the negroes and poor whites, had a problem similar to, though not so large as, that of India. In the Southern United States the Rockefeller Foundation went in and studied conditions. It discovered remedies and published the results in the "General Education Board's Report of the Rockefeller Foundation." The Foundation was kind enough to let me have five hundred copies of this valuable document. These were distributed widely to Government officials, prominent Indians and missionaries. Not a little credit for the wonderful forward strides taken in the last four years in India is due to this American literature.

This literature describes the functions of the farm demonstrator and county adviser. It shows how these trained men went to the debt-laden, hopeless farmer of the South and showed him on his own land, with his own labor, how to grow crops which surprised the farmer himself, put him out of debt and brought new hope to him.

If America can give to India a few missionary institutions like Hampton or Tuskegee, co-educational, properly staffed with enough adequately trained Americans, she will do India an inestimable service. In such institutions some Indians can be trained to farm their own land for a much larger profit than they now get per acre, other men can be trained as demonstrators to go to the debt-laden, hopeless and despondent Indian farmer, and further, the right kind of teacher can be trained for the rural schools. The demonstrator proves to the cultivator that "book farming" is profitable. As a result the farmer wants his children educated, and, as a result of his larger crops, he is able to pay for his children's education. Great Britain does not have the conditions which call for such institutions. As I go about America many say to me:—"Yes, what you say about India is interesting, but after all what business have American Missions in India? India is Great Britain's job." Frankly I admit that American Missions have no "business" in India and that no legal claim can be made upon American Christians to send help to India. It is only in the abundance of America's good-will, of her resources, of her conspicuous ability to help, and finally in her obedience to the command of Christ to go to the uttermost parts of the earth that justify her in giving this assistance to India. Even in my copy of the American revised version it does not say to American Christians "Go ye into all the world except the British Empire." India's need, America's ability to meet that need in relation to the command of Christ, is America's reason for sending of her sons and daughters to help this great and ancient people to gain the fullest measure of human freedom, and to learn the peace of God which passeth understanding. The reason I advise that so many properly qualified Americans be sent out is not that India's own sons and daughters are not capable, but they have not had the chance for training in India which they need and which America has. Other things being equal, the greater the number of American helpers as a temporary measure, the quicker India will be able to manage her own affairs.

After I had made a study of the problem of mission industries and saw they must be an essential part of the missionary method, I decided to choose agriculture in preference to anything else for the following reasons:

1. Agriculture is to-day the main occupation in India. It is the basic industry of the world.

2. Agriculture is likely to remain the main occupation of India, because of its climate and the long growing season.

3. Improved agriculture is the line of least resistance in a society bound by caste and may be the line of greatest wisdom. It is the simplest and most direct way to give India enough to eat and to prevent famine.

4. Improved agriculture, taught to the low-caste convert will give him enough to eat and will provide him with a surplus with which he can purchase clothing, pay the doctor, educate his children and contribute reasonably to the support of his religion. He learns by his own efforts how to support himself and his family.

5. Improved agriculture provides an occupation for sons of Christians who are not fitted to be mission teachers or preachers. Hitherto the main efforts of mission training have been directed toward the keeping up of the supply of evangelists and teachers. Not all good Christians are called of God to these forms of service. Since mission service is a form of life insurance for the time server, many have entered into this form of Christian work who were not suited either by their aptitude or their consecration to teaching or preaching. Because there was no other form of training provided by the mission a class of professional religionists has been fostered who are not always a credit to their mission or to Christianity. The boy who is trained in agriculture has no difficulty in obtaining a good job apart from the mission, often at a salary much higher than the mission could afford to pay. We have had men, trained on the farm at Allahabad, who deliberately chose mission service at a lower rate of pay, rather than other employment at a higher salary be-

cause they felt that in the mission they might help their own people better than by earning a big salary for themselves elsewhere. This raises the Indian to the same status as the missionary himself, who serves not for what he can get but for what he can give to others. This opens another possible occupation for Indian Christians and the more of such properly trained men there are, the sooner will the Indian be the real leader of his own people in their long struggle out of economic bondage into economic freedom.

6. The fact that so few low-caste folk possess land has been used as an argument against mission agricultural training. What is the good, our critics ask, of training men in this profession when they have no land of their own or are unable to rent land? The answer is, that even illiterate low-caste non-Christians, who have worked on the mission farm for two or three years and who have learned how to use iron plows, harrows, rollers, seeding, mowing and threshing machinery and silage cutters, are in great demand at wages two and one-half times as great as the average village wage. We have never had difficulty in getting eager laborers who wish to improve their own condition by getting practical training with us which fits them for higher wages elsewhere.

7. When I first came into contact with the non-Christian student of an Indian college, I was interested to find out what he was going to do with his education. I discovered that a very large majority were looking forward to Government service. In fact for every Government post which fell vacant about a hundred students applied. The ninety and nine who failed to obtain the post fed the ranks of the embittered and made Indian unrest more

widespread. They asked, "Why did the Government accept our fees for educating us and then not give us jobs?"

Failing Government services, the law is their second choice, and India, though possessed of some good, great, constructive and clever lawyers, has far more men in this profession than the country needs. If they fail in law, things have come to a bad pass, and there is nothing left but teaching in a Government school, or failing this, in a mission school, or a clerkship on the railroad or in a mercantile house. But in any one of these occupations life can never have the glory and honor it would have had in Government service.

Only a small minority go out into life looking for responsibility or for public service or to see how much good they can do.

There are a few who do not feel like accepting any post under Government since in such a position they would be prevented from criticizing its policy or questioning its action in any way. They prefer their independence and poverty to a post in a Government "machine" where there is the assurance of a fair salary, leading to a comfortable old age with a good pension. The number of occupations open to educated Indians which allow them to preserve their independence are very few.

In choosing agriculture I felt that a training in it would give the educated non-Christian Indian opportunity to earn a decent livelihood, and to keep his own independence and self-respect. If a large body of such men could be created in India to-day they would be of great assistance both to the Government and the people. As a class they would not be so bitter as the present dis-

appointed candidates for Government service, nor so
pliant and servile as some of the successful so often are.
They could be of great service in providing an educated
Indian public opinion free from prejudice.

8. There is a great call to-day for more technical and
industrial education in India. Some urge the Government to press on with this to the exclusion of all else.
The patriotic Indian does not like to see India so dependent upon other countries for the very simplest
manufactured necessities such as matches, lamps and
tools. He wants the Government to subsidize in some
way all Indian manufacturers. One great reason
against this, is that India to-day has so small a proportion of her population that can use tools and manage
machines, the lack of trained machinists could not be
overcome for years. I would be the first to agree that
India needs a greater proportion of her people engaged
in manufacture and industry and fewer in agriculture.
I feel that this can best be brought about by the development of those industries related to and subsidiary to
agriculture such as:

> The making and repairing of modern farm imple-
> ments and machinery.
>
> Modern dairying.
>
> The canning, and preserving, and drying of fruits
> and vegetables.
>
> Sugar making.
>
> Oil pressing.
>
> Tanning.
>
> Rope making.

To illustrate how improved agriculture helps the industries I speak of, on the land of the mission farm

where, before we took it, one blacksmith and one carpenter were occupied for less than half their time, after the mission took it and introduced labor-saving machinery, two blacksmiths and two carpenters have steady work all the time, keeping our machines in working order, and setting up new machinery for purchasers.

The limiting factor to-day to the introduction of modern, efficient, labor-saving farm machinery into India is not money, but lack of men trained to use modern farm tools and to keep them in repair. India has several million wells in areas where there never can be flow irrigation. At present the water is raised by bullocks, a slow and expensive method. The engineer who can overcome all the difficulties and give to India a cheap, durable, efficient and simple well-pumping outfit will do a great thing for India. We therefore wish to establish a strong agricultural engineering department to remedy this obvious lack.

9. The present system of rural and primary education is not popular in India largely because it is not vocational or "dollar" education, it is too literal, too detached and unrelated to the life of the people, but even more so because the boy who succeeds in it is lost to his village and to his own people. If he succeeds he is drawn away to the cities. India is a land of peculiar rural type. Over ninety per cent. of the population live in small villages and less than ten per cent. in cities and towns. The large cities of India, for a country with such a teeming population are very few.

Calcutta .... 1,200,000 inhabitants approximate
Bombay .... 1,100,000 inhabitants approximate
Madras ....   500,000 inhabitants approximate

Lahore ....
Delhi ....
Agra ....
Lucknow .... } from   200,000 to 400,000
Allahabad ....
Poona ....
Benares ....

Including these cities there are only seventy-five towns
and cities with over fifty thousand population each.
Men trained as farmers will do their work and earn
their living among their own people in the villages.
Each properly trained farmer will be as a light on a
hill to all the ordinary village farmers. He will use and
introduce the better seed, methods and implements.
When his neighbors see the better yields his practices
will be noted and copied by them. This will raise the
yield of the crops and the standard of living for all. I
believe this is the quickest way to reach the whole of
India helpfully, naturally and economically.

10. India needs roads, railroads, canals, schools, colleges, libraries, and hospitals. Sixty-two per cent. of
the people of India are beyond the reach of any medical
aid whatsoever. India is so poor that she cannot in her
present condition provide the capital for a large part,
much less, for all of these things. Such blessings are not
going to be given to her as an act of charity by any other
people. If she ever gets them it will be by her own efforts. The only possible place that I can see that she
can get them is from the first foot of her own soil, properly tilled. By the present old fashioned and inefficient
methods, India out of one of the richest soils on the earth
has the smallest yield per acre or per man of any civilized country. So the rapid introduction of better farming is the most natural and easy method of giving to

India the things of which she stands so sorely in need. This is the one sure way to rid India of the ever present nightmare, as well as the reality, of famine, and from the missionary standpoint the one sure way to get the self-supporting, self-propagating, self-governing church.

Better farming for India means the introduction of modern machinery adapted to Indian conditions. The Indian farmer has gone about as far as any one can go with implements made of bamboo tied together with weak string; to get bigger crops he must have better tools. The present tools and implements do not call out from the user any large degree of intelligence. It is for this reason that mission farms using Indian tools and methods have not made any substantial progress. But the Indian boy who learns to care for a tractor, or a threshing machine, or a silage cutter, knows he has learned something that calls for more brains and effort. Modern machinery challenges the Indian farmer boy just as it has the American farmer boy.

"Give ye ear, and hear my voice; hearken, and hear my speech. Doth he that ploweth to sow plow continually? doth he continually open and harrow his ground? When he hath levelled the face thereof, doth he not cast abroad the fitches, and scatter the cummin, and put in the wheat in rows, and the barley in the appointed place, and the spelt in the border thereof? For his God doth instruct him aright, and doth teach him. For the fitches are not threshed with a sharp threshing instrument, neither is a cart wheel turned about upon the cummin; but the fitches are beaten out with a staff, and the cummin with a rod. Bread grain is ground; for he will not be always threshing it: and though the wheel of his cart and his horses scatter it, he doth not grind it. This also cometh forth from Jehovah of hosts, who is wonderful in counsel, and excellent in wisdom."

Isaiah 28:23–29. Am. R. V.

CHAPTER V

HOW THE FARM STARTED

In going into these mud villages one not only learned that India was poor beyond compare, "cabined, cribbed, confined" by caste, and illiterate to an appalling extent; but also that India was a land where one occupation overshadowed all others. That occupation was farming. The census figures give sixty-five per cent. engaged in agriculture proper, and fifteen per cent. in looking after cattle, working in forests or in working as casual landless laborers on the farms of India. Thus eighty per cent. of the population of India gets its living from the soil. India will remain predominately agricultural largely because of the climate.

For the four months from November to March Northern India where Allahabad is located has a delightful climate, sunny days, starlit nights, little or no rain, the thermometer occasionally registering frost at night and rarely rising beyond 90° F. at noon. This is the season when there is a riot of flowers; roses, violets, heliotrope, chrysanthemums, pansies, oleanders, poinsettias and many others add color and odor that enrapture the lover of a good garden. The best American vegetable seeds give results of a kind that is rarely attained in America. March is a month of transition. In April the weather begins to warm up, May and June are called the "hot weather" months and have a shade temperature from 105° to 118° F., sun temperatures from 160° to 180° F. There is a hot wind from the west known as the "Loo." It is dangerous to be out of doors in the "Loo." The Indian is afraid of it, many die from its effects. About July first the "monsoon bursts" or "the rains break" and Allahabad is due to receive forty inches of rain in the following three months. The rain seldom comes in gentle well-timed showers, but often in a series of cloud bursts. On August 9th, 1919, fourteen inches fell in eight hours at Sutna which is about a hundred miles south of Allahabad. On August 13th, 1919, an area of over forty thousand square miles in extent received over four inches in twenty-four hours. On July 9th, 1920, Allahabad had eight and twenty-four hundredths inches of rain. I have measured on our farm a fall of four and a half inches in forty-five minutes. All roads, bridges, culverts, railway enbankments have to be built with such abnormal rainfall in mind. Between these heavy downpours we are apt to have "breaks" in the rains. Several days perhaps, sometimes several weeks, as in 1918, may pass without a drop of rain falling. The air is often saturated to such an extent that linen after absorbing moisture from the air can be wrung out as though it had been dipped in water. Humidity at Allahabad:

	1920	
July 9th	10th	11th
96	93	98

Saturation 100

COLD WEATHER CHART. I

THE WEATHER

METEOROLOGICAL OBSERVATIONS

Recorded at Allahabad

Week Ending Jan. 28, 1920	22nd	23rd	24th	25th	26th	27th	28th
Barometer reduced to 32°F.	29.863	29.807	29.824	29.788	29.780	29.806	29.645
Temperature of the air	51.5	51.5	51.4	54.5	55.7	55.3	51.2
Humidity (saturation = 100)	72	83	83	83	67	53	55
Wind direction..	CALM	CALM	CALM	CALM	W.	WSW.	W.
Maximum temperature in shade	75.2	76.5	76.5	80.2	81.0	79.2	74.2
Minimum temperature in shade	43.4	44.5	47.6	48.5	49.9	47.4	42.9
Mean temperature of the day	59.3	60.5	62.0	64.3	65.4	63.3	58.5
Normal temperature of the day	60.7	60.8	60.8	60.6	60.9	60.7	60.7
Rain	0	0	0	0	0	0	0
Total rain from 1st January ..	0	0	0	0	0	0	0
Normal total up to date	0.48	0.52	0.57	0.62	0.66	0.68	0.70

N. B.—The normal temperature and rainfall of each day are derived from the observations of 28 years, 1870–98.

Quoted from the *Pioneer Mail*, January 30, 1920.

TYPICAL HOT WEATHER CHART. II

THE WEATHER

METEOROLOGICAL OBSERVATIONS

Recorded at Allahabad

Week Ending June 9, 1920	3rd	4th	5th	6th	7th	8th	9th
Barometer reduced to 32°F.	29.329	29.331	29.302	29.257	29.237	29.244	29.232
Temperature of the air	94.0	96.7	93.7	90.3	95.5	94.0	93.4
Humidity (saturation = 100)	36	32	37	39	35	48	51
Wind direction..	WSW.	W.	CALM	W.	CALM	E.N.E.	E.

Maximum temperature in shade	108.4	108.0	109.9	112.3	107.6	113.5	113.7
Minimum temperature in shade	81.2	81.5	83.5	86.9	83.5	86.2	87.2
Mean temperature of the day	94.8	94.7	96.7	99.6	99.5	99.8	100.4
Normal temperature of the day	94.3	94.5	94.1	93.6	93.5	94.0	93.8
Rain	0	0	0	0	0	0	0
Total rain from 1st January ..	1.33	1.33	1.33	1.33	1.33	1.33	1.33
Normal total up to date	2.08	2.12	2.18	2.24	2.36	2.66	2.44

N. B.—The normal temperature and rainfall of each day are derived from the observations of 28 years, 1870–98.

This shows 1.33 inches of rain in six months.

The maximum sun temperature would be 160°–180°.

Quoted from the *Pioneer Mail*, June 11, 1920.

RAINS

THE WEATHER. CHART III

METEOROLOGICAL OBSERVATIONS
Recorded at Allahabad

Week Ending July 14, 1920	8th	9th	10th	11th	12th	13th	14th
Barometer reduced to 32°F.	29.212	29.196	29.204	29.170	29.148	29.199	29.181
Temperature of the air	83.6	80.7	80.4	79.0	82.0	80.3	80.4
Humidity (saturation = 100)	81	96	93	98	93	95	93
Wind direction .	ENE.	CALM	WSW.	NNW.	ENE.	WSW.	W.
Maximum temperature in shade	94.9	94.0	89.0	83.2	83.4	87.6	86.4
Minimum temperature in shade	80.0	78.3	80.0	78.4	78.6	78.8	77.9
Mean temperature of the day	87.4	86.1	84.5	80.8	81.0	83.2	82.1
Normal temperature of the day	85.3	85.2	85.2	85.3	85.3	85.4	85.3
Rain	0	8.24	0.11	1.54	1.87	0.33	0.26
Total rain from 1st January ..	2.98	11.22	11.33	12.87	14.74	15.07	15.33
Normal total up to date	10.73	11.07	11.39	11.68	11.94	12.16	12.43

N. B.—The normal temperature and rainfall of each day are derived from the observations of 28 years, 1870–98.

Quoted from the *Pioneer Mail* of July 16, 1920.

A moldy Bible or moldy pair of shoes during this season is no particular discredit to their owner. The humidity is very favorable to the growth of molds of every kind. This also is the season of prickly heat and boils, both of which need strong counter-irritants in order that the mind may be diverted from them. During the hot season and the rainy season the effort to keep alive absorbs most of one's energies. Under such conditions, which, with some variations, are common to the "plains" of India, mill and factory life with their regular hours, hard, confining work, have little attraction for the Indian. Every large non-agricultural industry in India has great difficulty in obtaining an adequate supply of labor. Until the general standard of living be raised an increase in wages may result only in the workman working fewer days in the month. Increase of money is not so necessary as a "divine discontent" with his present standard. An increase of desire must precede any rise in the standard of living.

Not only is the climate against mill and factory life but the fact that in India the growing season for crops lasts for twelve months as against six months per year in the northern United States also favors Indian farming. In late October and early November wheat, barley, peas, mustard, linseed, potatoes and vegetables are sown. These crops are reaped normally before April 10th. Sugar cane is sown from January to March, reaped and crushed from December to March, cotton sown from March to July is picked from August to December. The fodder crops, which include sorghums, millets, maize, and pigeon peas and the seeds of the castor oil plant and the plant family which includes watermelons, cucumbers, and squash are sown with the coming of the rains and the produce is gathered or reaped from October to May. So wherever there is irrigation there can be a very fair distribution of agricultural labor over the whole year. In spite of the great variety of staple crops the yields per acre and per man in India are lower than in any other civilized country. Rothampstead in England is the mother of agricultural experiment stations. On one plot for over seventy years without manure wheat has been grown continually year after year. The average yield per acre of wheat for the whole of India is less than the famous unmanured plot, wheat after wheat, at Rothampstead. On comparing the large and profitable yields of crops in the jail with the pitifully small yields of the villagers' plots, I approached certain government officials and missionary bodies and said: "In view of the present condition in India and the great need for more food and education, surely, if Government and missions are justified in carrying on any kind of education, they are justified in establishing that kind of education which most directly meets the needs of the great majority of the people of India." For a time no one would pay any attention, but I still continued to gather facts and figures and to present them to my friends. Every kind of objection was urged in favor of the status quo; the fact that Indian civilization was already old when our own ancestors were still barbaric savages; the fact that every possible or conceivable contingency in the Indian agricultural year was treated of in a beautiful rhyming Sanskrit couplet did not impress me, when I compared the poor Indian villager who seldom had enough to eat and the people of my own country, who, lacking the ancient civilization and the Sanskrit couplets, still had enough and to spare.

Finally the Mission authorities said: "Well, if you think we ought to be teaching scientific, modern farming, as a missionary method, why do you not return to America and study the subject and see if the folk in America will back your faith with their money?" In March, 1909, I left Allahabad and went to the Ohio State University to study agriculture. For the next two years, in addition to studying in the University, I made on the average of thirty missionary addresses each month, in churches, schools, colleges, theological seminaries, clubs. Sometimes the response was touching. After the Laymen's Missionary meeting in the great auditorium of Chicago, a scene shifter, all grimy and in his shirt sleeves, pressed a soiled ten dollar bill in my hand, saying, "Take this and use it for me over there." Some of the boys at one of the reformatories gave all their savings. A little two dollar and a half gold piece was given me by an aged lady in Staunton, Virginia, the birthplace of President Wilson. It had been presented to her by her lover who was killed in the Civil War, and was all she had left to remind her of him. Another woman from the Pacific Coast sent me a five dollar gold piece, the first earnings of her son who had recently died of tuberculosis. Some large gifts came also, but most were in sums under ten dollars.

There was also a response in the dedication of life. I have shaken hands in India with five women missionaries who had attended my first mission study class on India at the Lake Geneva Student Conference in 1909. It was a great privilege to coöperate with the Student Volunteer Movement in recruiting for the foreign field. Many nights each month were spent on sleeping cars, and by overnight journeys from Columbus I spoke in such centers as Washington, New York, Chicago, Rochester, Philadelphia, Cleveland and Cincinnati. It was hard, exhausting work, especially as for nine months I suffered with severe attacks of malaria brought with me from India. But, the thought of the need of the India that I loved, to which God had called me, gave me a strength beyond my own.

I was graduated B. Sc. in Agriculture in June, 1911, and returned to India in October, 1911, with thirty thousand dollars of real money given by friends who believed in this form of evangel. With the thirty thousand dollars given by friends in America, two hundred and seventy-five acres of land in one solid block were purchased for about eleven thousand dollars. In order to secure this land for an agricultural college it was necessary to appeal to the government to put the Land Acquisition Act into force. This it was kind enough to do to secure the land, but the Mission paid for it. The old Jumna Mission compound, which has been in possession of the Mission since before the mutiny, contains the Ewing Christian College and the boys' high school. It occupies a beautiful site on the north bank of the Jumna river, having about one-third of a mile of river frontage. The Jumna river at Allahabad varies in width from a half mile during the cold season to about a mile during the rains. The college campus goes right up to the two story bridge which carries the main line of the East Indian Railway on the upper story with a cart track underneath the railway. Across the bridge and immediately opposite the college campus is the Mission farm. This gives a most desirable and beautiful location for a college campus and agricultural institution. The land selected for the farm was rough, and very badly eroded and cut up into gullies. There were a great many small, irregular shaped fields. The land, having been deposited by the river in flood time, consists of nearly every kind of soil found in Northern and Central India, ranging from nearly pure sand through the loams to the clays and some patches of the characteristic "black cotton" soil of Central India. A good deal of this land had not been plowed within the memory of man. It was very badly infested with two grasses both of which have underground stems. When this land was plowed with the little Indian plow it cut across these underground stems and every place the plow broke the underground stems a new clump of grass came up so quickly that no seed that the Indian farmer could sow could get a sufficient start to keep ahead of these grasses. The grass would choke out anything planted in it. The Indian cultivator cannot plow this land except under the most favorable conditions. During the dry season of the year the ground is so hard that his little plow will not get in to break it so he has to wait until the rains have sufficiently softened it to enable his little plow to scratch the surface. In 1912 when I was down with typhoid fever my colleagues tried to rent some of this land to the farmers, but they would not give eight cents an acre for some of it. I knew that this land was very poor and difficult to cultivate. That was one of the reasons that I chose it. If I had chosen a good piece of rich, level land, irrigated from the canal, the Indian farmer would have said that anybody could farm and get a living on good land like that. I chose this poor land, eroded and full of pest plants difficult to eradicate, in order to show that the millions of acres of such land in Northern India could be redeemed and made profitable. Another reason for choosing this land was its location, so near the college and the city. Allahabad is the capital of the United Provinces which have a population of about fifty millions. At some time or other the leaders of these Provinces come to the capital city. The farm being on the river bank, overlooked by the railway, and having two of the main roads into Allahabad pass by it, is in a commanding position for a demonstration farm. Being so near the city provided a market for the dairy products and surplus vegetables. Furthermore, during the Hindu month, Magh, from the middle of our January to the middle of February, Allahabad is the greatest pilgrim center on earth. On some of the big days of the Mela, crowds of from two to four million pilgrims gather to bathe in the sacred waters of the two rivers which are seen, the Ganges and the Jumna, and the river Saraswati, the river that can only be seen by the eye of faith, that is said to flow underground for hundreds of miles and joins the sacred Ganges at this hallowed spot. Where these three sacred waters unite great benefit is supposed to accrue to the one bathing under the right auspices during this month, Magh. Hundreds of thousands of these pilgrims each year walk past the Mission farm. Many stop to see our improved tools and implements, our sleek, well-fed cattle, our silos and sanitary barns. They carry the tidings to the most remote parts of the Indian Empire. We get many inquiries about the purchase of machinery from far away places where these pilgrims have told of what they have seen.

I have said that this land was badly infested with weeds, thorns and grasses. The Indian tools and implements could not eradicate them, but we, with our American Titan tractor with three American plows behind it, or a Spaulding deep-tilling tool, drawn by six pairs of oxen, could go into these fields when they were hard and dry and thoroughly open them up, destroy the hard pan, the impervious layer, just below where the Indian plow could reach. When the land was thus plowed, the hot, scorching sun dried out all the stems and roots of the grasses which had been turned up and these when dead improved the soil. Being possessed of implements which could master it we succeeded in cleaning the land by this deep hot-weather plowing. We are raising large fodder crops, and grain and oil seeds on land which eight years ago would not rent for eight cents per acre. The farmers that refused eight cents eight years ago offered last year, 1919, seven dollars per acre rent for the same land, because they said we had so cleaned it and increased its fertility that it would produce crops enough to pay the big rental. Improved implements are a necessity if the yield of crops in India is to be increased.

My colleague, Mr. Bembower, has laid out vegetable gardens and orchards of mango, orange and guava.

After purchasing the land the rest of the thirty thousand dollars was spent in building one six-room bungalow; building a cattle shed two hundred and forty feet long by twenty-four feet wide; in putting in underground silos, building a store room and shed for tools, implements and grains, in purchasing dairy cattle and work oxen, a flock of sheep and goats, buying wire fencing, putting in roads and paths, improving our wells so that we were sure of an abundant supply of water for the cattle and the people. A number of implement makers in America gave us tools. In most cases these have led to business from Indians who have seen the things working on the Mission farm. The thirty thousand dollars,

however, was all spent before we had any dormitory,
class-room or laboratory accommodations. We urgently
need a laboratory and houses for our teachers. The
first students who came to us were poor Christian boys.
My wife gave the back verandah of the six-room bungalow and part of the dining-room for a dairy. I filled the
guest-chamber with our good seed and used the front
verandah as our recitation room. The students slept out
when the weather permitted, and when it did not, they
went in under the cattle shed or the machinery store
room. I was very glad indeed to receive from Mrs.
McCormick, of Chicago, five thousand dollars to build the
first wing of a dormitory. The very day on which Sir
James Meston (now Lord Meston), then Governor of the
Provinces, opened the dormitory a check came from Mrs.
Livingston Taylor for the other wing. Friends of the
late Mr. John H. Converse have provided the dormitory
body to which the wings are attached. Each one of
these buildings had students living in them before they
were finished. We have had to fit up some of these
small dormitory rooms as recitation and laboratory
rooms until we are fortunate enough to secure our laboratory. The local government has promised a grant-
in-aid of one-half the cost of a laboratory as soon as we
raise the other half.

With what equipment we had my colleagues and I
were training Indian boys, both Christian and non-
Christian. Many missionaries thought we were running a reformatory and were anxious to send those with
whom they could do nothing. At this time agricultural
education was not popular in India, the government
colleges could not secure enough students, the idea being
that any old fool knew how to farm and that there was

nothing that could be taught to the farmer from books. Gradually in India, as in America, the idea is taking hold that the farm, the ultimate source of food, as the supplier of food for the toilers in the busy cities is worth the best brains the country can produce. Some of the students of these early days are now rural secretaries for the Y.M.C.A.; some have received in addition to agricultural training, special training in rural economics and are now organizing rural coöperation societies among the outcastes; some are managing estates for large land-owners; some are members of our faculty; some are in charge of mission work in orphanages and schools; some are farming for themselves; some are working in Native States; and although some are neither a credit to themselves nor to the institution, yet I know of no other form of mission education in India where so many of those trained have put to the good of their fellows the training received and are a credit to the institution that trained them.

Harry Dutt was the son of an Indian Pastor, a nice boy but lazy. He felt that the Mission owed him an education. He had become parasitic in spirit. Owing to ill health he had not appeared to take his college entrance examinations, so could not go to college. I was urged to admit him to the Agricultural Institute, and finally, after much misgiving, consented. During the first year I watched him carefully, and at the end of it I called him to my office and said, ''Well, Harry, I have observed you carefully for this year and I have come to the conclusion that for your own good and the welfare of the institution, you had better make arrangements to go somewhere else for next year. I consider you thoroughly lazy. Your influence and example on the other students in bad, and we have no room for you here."

Harry seemed pained and surprised that I should so address him. He pleaded hard for another chance. I said, "What do you mean by another chance?" He replied, "Let me have a plot of land about as big as a farm around here, and I will be responsible for it, doing the work with my own hands, and if I am doing it alone you can then test my work in comparison with other students, and if I do not satisfy you, then turn me out." So I allowed him to return. He was given five acres of land for which he was charged rent. He was charged for the use of oxen and tools. Three days a week he attended lectures and laboratory. Three days he worked on his plot. He employed as general handy-man, cook and watchman, a little Christian hunchback. Harry drew up a plan for his plot, growing general field crops, and a vegetable plot, so as to grow most of the food he needed. He was so successful and hard-working that he soon had more vegetables than he could eat and his servant was taking the surplus to sell in the nearby village. Harry soon had money that he had earned by his own efforts in his pocket, and he held his head higher. He whistled as he worked; he had learned that by his own efforts he was sure of a good living. At the end of the year the books showed that he had made a net profit of twenty dollars an acre on land that previously had not yielded three dollars an acre net profit. This plot was one of the show places of the farm.

February of the next year, after the corner-stone laying of the great Hindu University at Benares six of India's Maharajahs, several of them in their own special trains stopped off at Allahabad to visit the Mission farm.

As I was showing one of these kings around he stopped

when he came to Harry Dutt's plot, so well laid out, clean, thrifty, with wonderful crops. His Highness said, "Whose plot is this?" I replied, "Harry Dutts.' Come here Harry. The Maharajah wants to speak to you." Harry stepped forward and answered a lot of questions. Then the Maharajah said, "Well, Harry, come and take charge of my palace gardens and I will pay you one-hundred and fifty rupees a month with allowances." Harry looked at me and said, "What shall I say to His Highness?" I answered, "You must answer for yourself. You have your own life to live." He hesitated a moment, then said, "Your Highness, I thank you for your kind offer, but I think I had better finish my course before I accept a position." A few weeks later I received a letter from Mr. Ray Carter, of Moga, who had started the school for training low-caste converts to go out as village teachers to their own people. Mr. Carter felt that it was necessary for these teachers to have a knowledge of better farming and so wanted to add an Agricultural Department to the school. In his letter Mr. Carter asked if we had any Indian Christian student well enough trained to take charge. I called Harry Dutt to my office and read Mr. Carter's letter to him, and said, "Now, Harry, what do you think of this for next year?" He replied that he had the Maharajah's offer to consider. I advised him to think of both. He took ten days' leave to go to both the King's palace and the Mission School to look the jobs over. When he returned he walked into my office and told me that he had accepted the position in the Mission School at Moga at seventy-five rupees a month. I asked him why he had accepted the Mission job on half the pay the Maharajah would have given.

He said, "Sir, you remember that day you threatened to expel me because I was lazy? I was very angry with you for speaking to me the way you did, but after thinking it over, I felt that you, a foreigner, were trying to do something to help my people, and I was hindering you, so I decided I would not be outdone by a foreigner. I too would give my life to help my own Christian people. I have accepted the lower salary in the Mission School because I feel I can help my own people better there than by accepting the larger salary and easier work with Maharajah."

When I was about to return to America, the Institute was short-handed, and we were looking round for some one to assist us. My colleagues unanimously agreed that we ought to invite Harry Dutt back to teach. One of the last pictures I saw of Harry Dutt was one in which he was teaching several young princes how to use the Planet junior wheel hoe.

After we got fairly started, the Crown Prince and his younger brother and four companions from one of the oldest and most influential states in India came for training in farming and since that time we have usually had some relative of one of the most ancient Indian royal houses among our students. We are teaching not only those from the bottom but those from the top. I consider that if these young nobles, many of whom will occupy positions of great power, understand the fundamental relation of larger crops to the betterment of India a great forward step will have been taken.

In the Allahabad district there are sixty-two village schools, generally in charge of a middle-aged or elderly gentleman who has never done a day's manual work in

his life. His salary ranges from three to six dollars a
month. When the British official in charge of the district, the Honorable Mr. S. H. Freemantle, C.I.E., read
of what had been done in the southern states of America
by the Rockefeller Foundation, and in the Philippine Islands by the United States, he arranged that every
school should have a fenced-in school garden. We had a
special summer school for these village teachers and
while not much agriculture could be taught in ten days
to these men, it was wonderful to see how their whole attitude of mind toward the importance of agriculture was
changed, and with what enthusiasm they went back to
their village schools. We have had two or more of these
Government teachers each year taking a special two
years' course in practical agriculture suitable for school
garden work. The most important part of the work the
Mission Agricultural School has done in India, is not
the very few small things which it has done of itself, but
the fact that it has aroused interest and called attention
to the fact of India's need of better farming and has
caused other people to do very much more than we ourselves could have done. Being a mission institution
every student, Christian or non-Christian, attends a daily
Bible class because the institution believes that it is not
better plowing or larger crops that is going to save India,
important as they are, but a faith which comes from
knowledge of Jesus, the world's Saviour. It is not that
we want men to change their religion just for the sake
of changing it, but because we believe that in Jesus there
is the complete and adequate satisfaction for every
hunger of man whether spiritual or material, whether
for time or eternity.

"For every beast of the forest is mine, and the cattle upon a thousand hills. I know all the fowls of the mountains: and the wild beasts of the field are mine. If I were hungry, I would not tell thee: for the world is mine, and the fulness thereof. Will I eat the flesh of bulls, or drink the blood of goats? Offer unto God thanksgiving; and pay thy vows unto the most High: And call upon me in the day of trouble: I will deliver thee, and thou shalt glorify me."

Ps. 50: 10–15.

CHAPTER VI

THE CATTLE PROBLEM OF INDIA

There are over 260,000,000 domesticated horned cattle, including water buffaloes in India. This works out to sixty-five head of cattle to every hundred of the population. Hence in the densely populated areas there is a very keen economic competition between the human beings and the cattle for the produce of the soil. My observation leads me to believe that over ninety per cent. of these cattle are an economic loss to the country, that is, the cow does not pay her board in the milk and offspring which she gives, and the ox is of so little value that it does not pay to raise him. Over ninety per cent. of the cows of India give less than six hundred pounds of milk a year. In most parts of India a three year old ox can be bought for twenty dollars. The milk and food he ate in his first year was worth more than this. I estimate that the loss per animal per year for 225,000,-000 head is ten dollars each, or a total aggregate loss per year of $2,250,000,000.

The cow is the most sacred of all the gods of India. It is worshipped by the Hindu. Hence the remedy for the excess of cattle in the western world can not be applied in India. In the west this excess of cattle would be sent to the packing houses, but in India, except for the small number of cattle eaten by the Mohammedans and Europeans most of the cattle die of old age or disease. The solution of the cattle problem of India by the Hindu himself is one of the most important and necessary reforms of India. It is evident that being a Hindu religious question it is not for a non-Hindu to decide it, but as a student of economics it is left to one to point out that the enormous number of cattle which do not pay their way are a very serious economic drain to a country as poor as India. It is not more cattle but better cattle that India needs.

It is obvious how the cow and the sacred bull rose to their place of preëminence in India. The ox is the source of India's power whether it be pulling the plow, drawing the water from the well, treading out the grain or taking the produce to market. He is well nigh indispensable, and has no substitute. The ox can work in an average mean temperature of eight to ten degrees hotter than the horse can stand. With the very small holdings which obtain in the densely populated parts of India, power machinery is beyond the reach of the farmer and if he could afford it, his holding is too small to make its use profitable. Therefore the ox seems destined to remain the source of India's power. There are many more breeds of cattle in India than there are in Europe or America. Some of these breeds are unsurpassed for draft and speed. Some are of excellent beef type. There is no real first class dairy breed. The best

Indian animals give between five and seven thousand pounds per year as against the best dairy breeds of America giving between twenty and thirty thousand pounds of milk a year.

I account for the rise of the Brahamini bull to power in the following way. In the case of the failure of the rains it is the cattle that suffer the most severely. Owing to the failure of the rains in 1918 in the Ahmadnagar district eighty per cent. of the cattle died because there was no fodder. The Bombay *Times* of the fifteenth of August, 1919, reported that in the preceding year from fifty to sixty per cent. of the cattle had died in Scinde because of lack of fodder and lack of roads. These famines are so severe that unless special provision were made it would be quite possible over a very large territory, for every single animal to die. Thus special provision must be taken and many animals are kept by the temples and share in the offerings made to the priests.

In connection with many of the temples one of the acts of worship is for the worshiper to take hold of the brush at the end of the cow's tail, under instructions of the priest. These cattle around the temples have a chance to live even though all the other cattle round about die.

In the densely populated parts of India the farm is so small that it is impossible to keep many cattle. The farmer usually keeps only one cow in order to raise the work oxen to do his plowing and to provide a little milk. Under these circumstances the one farmer can not afford to keep a bull or if he did keep one, the other farmers would not be willing to pay for the use of the bull. Therefore the custom has arisen, usually in celebration of some domestic event, that as a thank offering, one of the villagers takes a bull calf to the priest and has the sacred brand stamped upon it and henceforth it is sacred. It is then turned loose. No one may tie it up and it goes into the fields or into the village eating at its own sweet will and is usually in very good condition. The trouble with this method of breeding cattle is that there is no control. I have investigated a good many cases where cows of a fair dairy breed were brought into a district. The daughters of these cows sired by a local sacred bull give from one-half to one-fourth of the milk that the mother gave, proving that these sacred bulls are often very inferior dairy-breeding animals. Oftentimes the bull calf thus sacrificed is deformed or very small in size or unsuitable for some other reason for making into a work ox, thus with inferior sires the breeding of the cattle seems to be progressively worse. In certain parts of India there are certain castes whose business it is to breed cattle and they are very careful not to allow a sacred bull into their herds and also to choose good sires. They keep up the standard of their own particular breed.

The cattle of India are in general much more docile and easily handled than western cattle. This may be from the fact that they are often regarded as members of the family from birth, in and out of the house at will. The placid, contemplative cow is the type that appeals very strongly to the Hindu religious mystic whose idea is to spend his time out in the forest away from man, contemplating, as the cow appears to be doing as she placidly chews her cud.

In Europe the man who formerly wished to perpetuate his name built a cathedral; in modern America he builds a University; in modern India he builds and maintains a "Gowshala" where the aged, deformed, sick and decrepit cows can be sure of being well cared for, until they die a natural death. Much more is being done in India by the Hindus to preserve the cattle than to preserve the sick, decrepit and ill-nourished men and women.

There are a number of breeds of water-buffaloes in India; some of which are no better than those found in the Philippine Islands or China. Some breeds are excellent dairy animals. The Delhi buffaloes weighing anywhere from fifteen hundred pounds to a ton, with short, intensely curled horns, often give six to seven thousand pounds of milk a year having seven and a half to nine per cent. of butter fat. In the Government Military Dairies where some attention is now being paid to the improvement of the dairy cattle of India a number of buffaloes have given over ten thousand pounds of milk a year of about eight per cent. butter fat. The buffalo is much more nervous than the cow and must be handled more gently. Their habit is to feed at night and in the day time lie in water with only the eyes and nose showing. There is one breed of buffaloes that has four perfectly formed quarters and only two teats. There are no rudimentaries or anything to suggest that two teats have been lost. They are a very fair milking breed and are worth investigation. I believe that the water buffalo of India has a future in the southern states of America, notably in Florida where there is an abundance of water with lots of roughage.

The cattle of India are usually hardy and resistant to disease. Most of the cattle of India are only slightly affected by foot and mouth disease and are immune to tick fever. Tuberculosis is very rare among them. For this reason they have proved themselves of use in Texas and other southern states, being crossed with our western breeds.

The Bikanir camels are said to be the finest in the world. The great help that the Bikanir Camel Corps gave in defending the Suez Canal and in pursuing the retreating Turks is a glorious chapter in the history of the Great War. The Bikanir sheep is one of the finest-wooled sheep known and is worth studying and developing. India is a land that has millions of goats. Some of these give as high as eight pounds of milk a day. Some of them give actually more milk than many of the cows.

The cattle problem of India cannot be solved until there is an adequate veterinary force with power to stamp out disease as was done in the Philippines. We must not forget however and disregard the fact that in the Philippines it was infinitely easier because there were a number of islands and segregation was easy, while India is a great continent and thus almost impossible to isolate and segregate. The bigness of the problem however is no reason why it should not be tackled. The longer the delay the greater the progressive economic loss to India.

It was seeing the importance of the cattle as the power of India that led me to make my first serious agricultural study the means to safe-guard this power. I came to the conclusion that the silo was the best single means. During the normal rains in India enormous quantities of fodder grasses grow, both cultivated and wild. If at this time earthen silo pits could be dug and filled with these grasses it would keep for years. These pits would be a fodder bank. If when the time of scarcity came this fodder bank could be drawn upon, millions of cattle that are now lost could be saved. Here again ignorance and illiteracy have stood in the way of such a simple and obvious reform as this. Furthermore in these silo pits a great deal of vegetation which the cattle will not eat normally can be turned into succulent fodder. The students of the Allahabad Agricultural Institute counted and named twenty-two weeds which the cattle would not eat green which were put into the farm silo pit, and at the end of two months were fed to the cattle and the dairy herd increased in milk production.

In the Old Testament a truly delectable land is described as ''A land flowing with milk and honey.'' Modern India has the same conception of physical and material blessedness. Yet as one gets to know India and sees its multitudes of cattle, one is struck by the great difficulty of getting reasonably pure milk. Dr. H. H. Mann of Poona, Mr. Carruth of Madras, Dr. Joshi of Bombay, Major Matson of Calcutta have all investigated city milk supplies in India and each speak of the very few samples of milk taken from the milk sellers that were pure, most of them adulterated from twenty to seventy-five per cent. with water. Now if the water with which the milk was adulterated were only pure water not so much harm would result, but often the water used to adulterate the milk is unclean. It is likely to be contaminated with sewage and is very dangerous to health. Many serious attacks of dysentery, cholera and typhoid have been traced to milk adulterated with dirty water. Because of the difficulty of obtaining pure milk in India the military authorities put in their own dairies to supply the troops with safe milk and of better quality. The milk is supplied to the troops in bottles, sealed with the standard cap and seal made in Chicago. It is the only bottle fastener I have ever seen that the Indian milkman could not tamper with. If the cost to the military for milk and butter be considered apart from anything else, the cost is rather high, but when the medical figures are considered along with the cost, the absence among the troops of enteric disease since the installation of the military dairies, it is then seen that many lives are saved annually by these military dairies. In addition to providing good milk and butter for the troops the military dairies, in an indirect way, are doing much to better the dairy industry in India. They set standards of cleanliness and sanitation. They are importing pure bred bulls of the noted dairy breeds, many of the offspring of which are sold at auction and eagerly bought by the India Gowala (the caste that looks after the cows) with the result that the Gowala is growing less and less satisfied with the poor yields of the Indian cow. The Gowala now wants better stock.

In our mission dairy farm we have had no trouble in disposing of all our milk, much of it goes to educated Indians of caste who appreciate it for their children. A Missionary's daughter at seven months old was one pound lighter than the day she was born. The doctor said it was due to bad milk. The mother said the Gowala brought the cow and milked it in front of her and she did not see how the milk could not be pure. The doctor said he could not see either, but the baby's lack of growth was because of bad milk causing dysentery. The mother brought the baby to live near our mission dairy and drove night and morning to get our fresh pure milk. At eleven months the baby was normal in weight and the last time I saw her she was a beautiful, well-grown child. We feel that we owe the life of at least one of our own children to the good, pure milk supplied by the mission dairy. The Government is very anxious for us to have a properly equipped dairy school where we can train Indians to go out to supply the Indian cities with pure milk. The medical authorities feel that a good supply of pure, clean milk for Indian cities would do much to reduce the high infant mortality. So we are anxious to get our dairy equipment as soon as possible to enable us to meet this urgent demand and a thoroughly trained dairyman who is not afraid of difficult problems.

"When heaven is shut up, and there is no rain, because they have sinned against thee; if they pray toward this place, and confess thy name, and turn from their sin, when thou afflictest them: Then hear thou in heaven, and forgive the sin of thy servants, and of thy people Israel, that thou teach them the good way wherein they should walk, and give rain upon thy land, which thou hast given to thy people for an inheritance. If there be in the land famine, if there be pestilence, blasting mildew, locust, or if there be caterpillar; if their enemy besiege them in the land of their cities; whatsoever plague, whatsoever sickness there be; What prayer and supplication soever be made by any man, or by all thy people Israel, which shall know every man the plague of his own heart, and spread forth his hands toward this house: Then hear thou in heaven thy dwelling place, and forgive, and do, and give to every man according to his ways, whose heart thou knowest; (for thou, even thou only, knowest the hearts of all the children of men;)

 *   *   *   *   *   *   *   *   *

Blessed be the Lord, that hath given rest unto his people Israel, according to all that he promised; there hath not failed one word of all his good promise, which he promised by the hand of Moses his servant. The Lord our God be with us, as he was with our fathers: let him not leave us, nor forsake us: That he may incline our hearts unto him, to walk in all his ways, and to keep his commandments, and his statutes, and his judgments, which he commanded our fathers."

I Kings 8: 35–39**56–57–58.

CHAPTER VII

THE BRITISH GOVERNMENT IN INDIA

I am frequently asked what the British government has done for India and why it does not do more. I hold no brief for the government and I can point out serious mistakes it has made. But others have written powerfully of these mistakes, while few have spoken of the positive, constructive side of British administration in India, so I shall confine myself chiefly to the credit side of the account. Among the things that the British have given to India is the system of law courts which recognizes all men as equals before the law. This, in a country of many religions and many languages, and above all of caste, is a very important thing.

India has a postal, money-order and telegraph system which is very much cheaper and better than the American. In 1914 a twelve word telegram could be sent anywhere in the Indian Empire for twelve cents, no zone system, one flat rate for the whole country. If the telegram were sent by cable from Aden which is five days' mail steamer journey from Bombay then across India by land, again under the Bay of Bengal by cable to Rangoon, it would be sent over three thousand miles. The postcard costs one-half cent, a sealed letter one cent. Five rupees ($1.66) or multiples of five rupees can be sent by money order for two cents for each five rupees.

The money-order form consists of four parts; one is retained by the office receiving the money, one is kept by the office distributing the money, one is kept by the man receiving the money and the fourth is returned to the remitter with the signature of the receiver and is considered a legal receipt.   Furthermore the postman actually brings the money to the person who is to receive it.   So there is not the waste of time going to the post office to get the money.   How much greater service is this than the modern American money-order service.   The postman also sells stamps and postcards on his rounds.

India has approximately thirty-six thousand miles of railroad, unfortunately divided between four gauges, five-foot-six-inch gauge, meter-gauge, two-foot-six-inch, and two-foot gauge.   No narrow gauge railway enters an Indian port, though the narrow gauge often serves a very rich and large district.   There is therefore a very great economic loss in the trans-shipment of goods from the various gauges.   Most of these railways were built with capital borrowed at a low rate of interest, none of it above six per cent. and most of it much below.   In order to induce capital to invest in Indian railroads the British government guaranteed the interest to the investors which the railway paid or not.   With the credit of the British government the Indian railways were thus built about as cheaply as any railroads on earth and the public in India gets the benefit.   The mail trains between Calcutta and Bombay, thirteen hundred miles, between Calcutta and Lahore, about the same distance, run at about thirty-three miles an hour for the whole of the distance.   The first class accommodation which equals if it does not excel the Pullman, costs between three and four cents a mile, second class about two cents, intermediate less than one cent and third class three miles for one cent. Had the railways of India been compelled to depend upon Indian capital for their building there would have been very great difficulty and fewer miles of road, for the Indian investor or money-lender, the Bania, is seldom satisfied with less than sixteen per cent. per annum but prefers from seventy-two to one hundred per cent. per annum. The history of famines in India is divided into two clearly marked portions, one before the coming of the railroads when famine in any district meant death to great numbers of the people and to cattle without any hope of relief. It is on record that Agra was having famine during which more than half of the people died. At Mainpuri, less than one hundred miles distant from Agra, grain was being sold at two pounds for a cent. Owing to the absence of roads or railroads everything had to be transported on pack oxen which made it a physical impossibility to transport enough grain, even over such a short distance, to save the people. (See Sir Theodore Morison ''The Industrial Equipment of an Indian Province.'') A hundred miles in those days under those conditions was at least a week's journey. To-day when famine occurs special rates are given on the railroads for the transporting of grain and fodder into the affected area and very few people die compared with the pre-railway period. ''Famine'' in India is not always understood in America. Seldom is there a time in India when there is not food enough to go around. In the same year one part of India may be breaking the record by a bumper crop and a short distance away there may be a total crop failure. The beginning of the agricultural year in India is the

beginning of the "rains," in Northern India about the
first of July.   If the rains fail, there is no work for the
farmer or for the very large number of casual landless
laborers. Without the rain the fodder crops can not
be grown, neither can the fields be prepared for the grain
crops which are grown in the cold season.   Therefore the
failure of the rains means the absence of work for twelve
months or until the next rains, and the absence of work
means absence of wages and the absence of wages means
absence of food, therefore starvation.   Indian merchants
are like any other merchants.   They do not see why, if
they deal in grain and pay their money for it, they
should not sell it at a profit.   They cannot see why they
should be compelled to give it away because somebody
else has not bought and stored it and cannot afford to
buy.   The grain merchant gets little sympathy when a
bumper harvest compels him to sell at a loss the grain
bought and stored with so much care.

India in general is remarkable for its generosity in
famine times.   The poor help one another with gifts of
grain.   Recognizing the true cause of famine, the British
government has drawn up a code which prescribes the
course to be followed in case of scarcity.   A large re-
serve fund has been accumulated for the purpose of
caring for the people during the famine.   Much government labor, digging of canals, the building of roads,
railways, bridges, clearing of forests, damming of rivers,
putting in storage reservoirs, is all undertaken as famine
relief work.   The policy is to pay wages lower than
market rates, so that as soon as conditions improve in
the country around about, the people will automatically
disappear from the famine relief works.   Thus private

enterprise will not suffer from lack of labor due to government competition. When there is no work in the
villages the people come to the famine relief work. As
soon as private enterprise can pay more than famine
work the private enterprise gets its labor. In addition,
to the land-owner, and to tenants having permanent
rights in the land, advances are made of money,
"Tacavi," long-term loans, usually at three per cent.
This money is to be spent for permanent improvements,
such as digging of wells with permanent masonry cylin-
ders or tile draining of land, the building of store rooms
of permanent material. One of the best ways to prevent
famine is to increase the irrigation facilities, for where
there is an abundant supply of irrigation water people
are indifferent to the amount of rainfall. As a result of
the irrigation system, large tracts that formerly were
desert and very precarious and uncertain are now secure
against any failure of the rains. The irrigation projects of India are divided into two classes, one protective,
the other productive. In the case of the protective irrigation project, the object is not to earn large dividends,
but the protection of the people in a famine year. In
parts of Central India which normally get sufficient rainfall, there is every four or five years a partial or total
failure of the rains when suffering and loss is very great.
Large irrigation works with storage reservoirs have been
put in. When there is a normal rainfall there is little
or no demand for the water which has been stored and
the project does not pay directly that year, but when
the rain fails, this water that has been stored, is used
and enables the country to tide over a bad time without
serious loss. The loss of water by surface evaporation is

not less than eight feet per year. So that to do any good these irrigation works have to have such large storage capacity that they are sometimes larger than seems necessary. One very interesting by-product of this large storage reservoir system is that there is a seepage and ground flow with a lateral movement of the water in the soil, so that wells five or six miles away from the storage reservoir that would have gone dry before the storage was put in, now have an abundance of water all through the dry season. These works are well named protective, and fully justify their construction.

In the case of the productive works there were large areas of good land in the region of deficient rain-fall in Northwest India including the Punjab where the slope was right and the rivers, the Jhelum, the Ravi, the Chenab, the Beas, the Sutlej and the Indus, bring down an abundance of snow waters from the Himalaya mountains which can easily be spread over the desert of the Punjab and cause it to blossom as the rose. Ten million acres are now thus irrigated and schemes are prepared for the irrigation of twelve million more acres. The Bhakra Dam project on the Sutlej will give 300,000 H.P. The height of the dam, 394 ft., will make it the highest in the world. The area that will be irrigated will be four times the irrigated area of Egypt.

"The value of the crops raised by the aid of the canal water during 1918 and 1919 was well over fifty-five crores of rupees (a crore is ten million rupees and the value of a rupee at that time was about forty-five cents), so the value of crops was $247,500,000. Had there been no canals it is safe to say that the area concerned would not have produced crops to the value of more than ten crores. The minimum new wealth created in a single year, was thus forty-five crores of rupees. The value of the year's crops amount to two and one-half times the total capital outlay on the whole canal system concerned. These productive canals earned in direct receipts a net return of 7.4 per cent. of which, after defraying interest charges, the net return was 4.96 per cent. The direct canal charges for water averaged Rs. 5.3 per acre of crop matured out of a gross value of Rs. 64 per acre of the crop grown." Quoted from *The Pioneer Mail* of June 18, 1920.

In the same year over nine million acres were irrigated and over twenty thousand miles of canals were operated in the Punjab alone and over fourteen million acres were irrigated by flow in the whole of India. It is safe to say that the government has charged to the cultivator a much lower water rate than a private concern would have done. It is hard to over-estimate the value of an irrigation system to a people. It gives a sense of security and certainty that nothing else does.

During the war the irrigation department went on and was very largely increased. It is estimated that two hundred and twelve million dollars have been invested by the government in irrigation in British India and it has still larger projects in hand. Not only is there promise of more water for irrigation but an abundance of water for hydro-electrical power. Notable examples are already in operation. The mills, factories, the street car lines of Bombay are run largely by water-power that falls down the Western Ghauts from thirteen to seventeen hundred feet in a sheer fall.

This is of very great importance when we remember that most of the coal used in Bombay is mined in Bengal and all during the war had to take an eleven hundred mile railway haul from the pit to Bombay at a charge of five dollars a ton freight.

The British have been accused of taxing India so heavily as to be the cause of India's poverty. Investigation shows that India is one of the least taxed countries on earth whether measured on percentages or by actual figures. The statement was recently made in the United States that the British took one-half of the produce of the soil in taxation. This is not the case. Such a statement arises out of a misunderstanding, a confusion between land revenue and produce of the soil. The different provinces of India have different systems of land tenure. A good many of these systems, like Topsy, have just grown. Bengal for instance has what is known as the "Permanent Settlement" where the landlords of Bengal and the government came to an agreement by which the amount of land revenue to be paid by the land-owner to the government was fixed for all time. The great omission in this agreement was that the amount of rent to be paid by the tenant to the land-owner was not fixed for all time. Whatever else the British have done or have not done for India, they certainly have brought peace. They have prevented the intertribal, internecine warfare. They have guaranteed to every man safety and protection. With the incoming of roads, railroads, water transportation, irrigation facilities, with the opening of Calcutta, so that to-day it is the largest port in Asia, great demand for the products of Bengal, its jute, rice, tea, indigo and pulses, have caused the population to increase rapidly. The result is an increased competition to secure land. Therefore while the land-lords in Bengal have been able to increase their rent at will to the tenant, the limit being only what the land-lord could squeeze out of the farmer, the amount he has paid to the government has remained fixed. The land-lord is the one who has received the lion's share of the unearned increment of the land. It has not been fairly divided. To-day all the other provinces of India are taxed to provide Bengal with money enough to run its government. Bengal has a large number of wealthy land-owners, many of them opulent profiteers, whose position has been strengthened by time. The injustice wrought through such an iniquitous contract falls very heavily upon the many, but the few who profit have never been willing to give up anything. The British government made a bad bargain for itself and has stuck to it, in order to keep its word.

In the United Provinces, which has an area of approximately one hundred thousand square miles, and a population of about fifty million people, there is a land-owner class and a tenant class. When the British entered this part of India, more often by contract than by conquest, they brought peace. In the old days the chiefs maintained themselves by strength of arms. The larger and better trained the fighting force of the chief the easier he could gobble up the smaller chief, and defend himself in case of attack. There was then great competition for the services of fighting men who were treated very generously by the chiefs, and given land on very favorable terms. When the British came in, ignorant of the real state of affairs, thinking the conditions were

similar to the conditions in England where there was
a large land-owning class, a yeoman class and farm-
laborer class, they confirmed the chief as land-owner and
the fighting man was considered the yeoman. With the
coming of peace the yeoman lost his value as a fighting
man which was due to the strong hand of the British
preventing the chiefs fighting among themselves. The
fighting man soon became little better than a serf. For
thirty years legislation has been enacted seeking to re-
store to the tenant farmer the rights which he had before the coming of the British. To-day there is a large
land-owning class, and two classes of tenant, one class
with permanent, inalienable rights to his land, the other
a tenant-at-will. The first class cannot be dispossessed
for any cause. He is a permanent tenant, a part owner.
This class forms sixty-six per cent. of the tenants. The
second class, the tenant-at-will, has no rights in the land.
He is usually not allowed to remain in possession longer
than one year. If he remains on the same piece of land
for two years, he gains these inalienable rights, hence
the landlord keeps him moving to prevent him acquiring
these rights of permanency. He forms thirty-three per
cent. of the tenantry, and is indescribably poor and im-
provident.

The government maintains a settlement department
where specially trained officers are sent once every thirty
years into a district, going into every field and deter-
mining in the presence of the landlord or his agent
and the tenant the amount which the permanent tenant
is to pay to the landlord. Of this sum paid by the
tenant to the landlord the Imperial government takes
fifty per cent. as land revenue while eight per cent. goes

in local assessments and taxation. Suppose the settlement officer decides that a given field shall pay annually
$1.00 per acre rent to the landlord, the government gets
fifty per cent. of the dollar, as land revenue. That particular field may grow a crop of sugar cane, turmeric
or potatoes where the net profit might easily be from
thirty to fifty dollars per acre. This sum fixed by the
settlement officer is the amount of rent which the tenant
with permanent rights must pay to the landlord. It
cannot be enhanced. In the case of assessing the land
of the tenant-at-will the settlement officer makes no
difference. He decides the land revenue as though all
tenants had permanent rights. For all the land held
under cultivation by tenants-at-will, the landlord can
charge as much rent as he can rack out of the tenant,
but he pays the government only fifty per cent. of the
amount determined by the settlement officer. For some
of this land assessed by the settlement officer to pay one
dollar per acre rent, the tenant-at-will pays as high as
ten dollars per acre. The government only gets fifty per
cent. of the assessed rental irrespective of the rent paid
by the tenant or the crop grown. The mistake in the
statement that the government takes fifty per cent. of
the produce of the soil, is made in confusing the amount
of the land-revenue with the total produce of the soil,
which are two entirely different things. The land-revenue seldom equals ten per cent. of the produce of the
soil and of that ten per cent. the government gets fifty
per cent. and the landlord forty-two per cent., eight
per cent. goes into local uses.

Again the government is criticized for taxing salt, a
necessity. The reason is, of course, that salt is the one

thing that catches everybody in India. It is necessary
for the government to raise money in order to carry on
a government. If it does not do it in one way it must
do it in another. In 1914 salt could usually be bought
at retail in India in the villages for one cent a pound
or one dollar a hundred pounds. The government tax
works out about forty cents to the hundred pounds of
salt. A man would use about one-half ounce of salt a
day or about one pound a month, twelve pounds a year.
In eight and a half years he would use about one hundred pounds of salt and in eight and a half years the
amount of salt he had used would pay the government
forty cents in tax. For the average life-time in India
the salt tax does not cause the individual to pay much
more than one dollar. The complaint of some of us in
India is not that the government taxes too much, but
that it does not tax enough. We feel that if it had taxed
more it would have had more money to spend on education, sanitation, irrigation, roads and other things which
India sadly lacks, and that are in reality investments of
public funds for the benefit of private citizens, and that
are cumulative in their effect on public welfare.

Much is said of the fearful drain of money on India to
support the army. Before the war about eighty-five thousand British and three hundred thousand Indian troops
were maintained in India for protection of the Indian
people. The Indian civil service has about one thousand
British men in it and the other services four or five
thousand. These highly trained men give the best years
of their lives for what may be considered not excessive
pay and are retired on a pension. Large sums of money
also leave India to pay the interest charges on the rail-

roads and irrigation schemes and other public utilities where the British lent their credit so that India could borrow money cheaply for all its public utilities. In each case it can be shown that whatever interest-money India pays outside of India, is paid for value received. Whether one nation is justified in ruling another is still an open question, and one can fully sympathize with the desire of the educated Indian to keep his own house. The British government has itself on record as deliberately planning for responsible government in India in the very immediate future, when every legislative council will have a majority of elected Indian members. To bring this about in the shortest possible time needs the very heartiest coöperation and good will between the educated Indian and the British government. It is not by constantly remembering the mistakes of the past of either side and brooding over them in a spirit of vengeance, but it is in looking to the future with a mutual trust and good will that promises the speediest fulfillment of India's desire for the fullest realization of her own genius in complete responsible government. Each has much to learn from the other, each has much to give to the other. Some may ask, if the Government of India is so good why is there any need for missionary effort? The same question may well be asked in the United States and the answer is the same. The government does not claim to cover the whole needs of the individual or social life. There is a limit to the causes for which public money may be spent. There is a certain "soullessness" to government which handicaps it and prevents its laying stress on certain needs of the people. It stands for the status quo. A government represents the people. It can go no faster than they will let it. The history of reform shows an individual in advance of a majority of his fellows, in advance of the government and often such an individual is a thorn in the side of a government which wants peace. A government is not equipped to experiment, and seldom takes up successful experiment. In the South it was Armstrong, Peabody, Miss Jeanes, The Rockefeller Foundation and others who have advanced and compelled the United States government to follow. In India Christian missions stand as the pioneers, the trail blazers. In most educational affairs the Indian government has followed the lead of the missionary, for example Carey and Duff, and in this day when all men everywhere are longing for the time when men shall beat their swords into plowshares and their spears into pruning hooks, in the day when agriculture and not war shall be supreme, it seems entirely fitting that the Christian missionary should maintain his place by demonstrating his fitness to lead India out of economic bondage into economic freedom, which is at the very foundation of all other freedom. Christian missions are spending about five million dollars on education in India. "India in 1919," page 133, says, "The contributions from missionary bodies and from charitable endowments is of rather greater importance than is indicated by its financial equivalent. Missionary bodies very often succeed in enlisting the services of devoted men whose ability is quite out of proportion to the remuneration which they are content to accept. Indeed Indian education, as a whole, owes to missionary bodies a debt which it is very difficult to estimate with justice."

Thus the government acknowledges its debt to the missionary and admits he has a place in the full, rounded, ordered development of India into a self-governing nation.

General Statement of the Revenue and Expenditure charged to Revenue, of the Government of India, in India and in England.

REVENUE

	Accounts, 1917–18	Revised Estimate, 1918–19	Budget Estimate, 1919–20
	£	£	£
Principal Head of Revenue.			
Land Revenue	21,607,246	20,805,900	22,686,400
Opium	3,078,903	3,229,000	3,056,200
Salt	5,499,487	4,216,300	3,914,300
Stamps	5,727,522	5,916,500	6,097,100
Excise	10,161,706	11,567,900	12,153,300
Customs	11,036,588	12,403,200	13,352,400
Income Tax	6,308,104	1,320,800	13,544,900
Other Heads	3,885,177	4,088,000	4,568,900
Total Principal Heads.....	67,304,733	69,547,600	79,383,500
Interest	2,170,108	3,842,900	3,637,400
Posts and Telegraphs.....	4,616,690	5,322,900	5,716,800
Mint	517,401	1,676,800	1,356,500
Receipts by Civil Departs...	1,935,364	2,086,600	1,957,500
Miscellaneous	4,868,356	5,924,300	2,557,400
Railways: Net Receipts ...	24,141,708	25,347,400	21,372,900
Irrigation	5,063,879	5,402,200	5,511,900
Other Public Works.......	323,599	321,900	323,000
Military Receipts	1,720,509	1,713,600	1,587,300
Total Revenue	112,662,347	121,186,200	123,404,200

Charts quoted from "India in 1919." Taken from between pages 57 and 58.

EXPENDITURE

	Accounts, 1917–18	Revised Estimate, 1918–19	Budget Estimate, 1919–20
	£	£	£
Direct Demands on the Revenues	9,854,695	11,669,900	11,293,300
Interest	7,328,169	7,866,600	7,763,500
Posts and Telegraphs	3,567,730	4,116,500	4,580,200
Mint	167,382	267,000	284,500
Salaries and expenses of Civil Departs.	20,855,368	24,233,500	24,549,100
Miscellaneous Civil Charges	5,918,797	6,257,400	6,139,100
Famine Relief and Insurance	1,000,000	1,000,000	1,789,100
Railways: Interest and Miscellaneous Charges	14,227,385	14,154,000	14,468,900
Irrigation	3,784,838	3,988,300	4,071,100
Other Public Works	5,048,294	5,582,100	6,932,700
Military Services	30,763,650	45,639,600	42,782,300
Total Expenditure, "Imperial and Provincial"	102,516,218	124,774,900	124,653,800
Add—Provincial Surpluses: that is, portion of allotments to Provincial Governments not spent by them in the year	2,256,623	1,091,000	. . . .
Deduct—Provincial Deficits: that is, portion of Provincial Expenditures defrayed from Provincial Balances	197,568	111,500	1,918,200
Total Expenditure charged to Revenue	104,575,273	125,754,400	122,735,600
Surplus	8,087,074	4,568,200	668,600
Total	112,662,347	121,186,200	123,404,200

"And when the queen of Sheba had seen all Solomon's wisdom, and the house that he had built, And the meat of his table, and the sitting of his servants, and the attendance of his ministers, and their apparel, and his cupbearers, and his ascent by which he went up unto the house of the Lord; there was no more spirit in her. And she said to the king, It was a true report that I heard in mine own land of thy acts and of thy wisdom. Howbeit I believed not the words, until I came, and mine eyes had seen it: and, behold, the half was not told me."

I Kings 10:4–7.

CHAPTER VIII

WORK IN NATIVE STATES

About one-third of the area of India but not one-third of the population enjoys home rule, that is, it is not directly under the British, but is ruled over by Indian kings or Rajahs. Within the native kingdoms the policy of the British is to interfere as little as possible. In general it is only when negotiations with other states or foreign governments are being carried on, that the British resident or adviser has anything to do, except in cases of gross and palpable misrule when the British government may suspend or dethrone the incompetent king and put up some other member of the ruling family who will give better government.

The size of these kingdoms varies. Hyderabad, a Mohammedan state, is 82,000 square miles in extent, slightly larger than Minnesota, with a population of 13,000,000, a large majority of whom are little better than serfs.

Jodhpur, famous as having given to the world the Jodhpur riding breeches which polo players and other horsemen wear, is 40,000 square miles in extent, about the size of Ohio, mostly desert. In Jodhpur are the famous white marble quarries from which the marble was taken across the desert to build the Taj Mahal at Agra, and how it was transported still remains a mystery.

Mysore, where the famous Kolar gold mines are, is

38,000 square miles in extent. Mysore is a very progressive state. Large hydro-electric power is being developed and used to foster industry. It has a well organized department of agriculture.

Gwalior is 28,000 square miles in extent, population 3,000,000, a country of marvelous possibility. The ruling family is Mahratta, one of the most famous warrior castes of Western India. As most of the state was won by conquests it is scattered and not in one continuous tract. It lies in larger or smaller patches roughly between the Nerbudda and Chambal rivers. It has some beautiful scenery. Water power and irrigation are being developed on a large scale. A tiger population of about four hundred, with leopard, panther, not-enumerated black bear, black buck and deer and wild pig in abundance.

Bikanir is 25,000 square miles, one solid block of desert. About one-third in the northern part will soon be under irrigation. I have never seen richer land and water will transform it into a wonderful garden spot. These are the largest and most important of the native states. In all, there are about seven hundred, ranging from larger than Minnesota down to the size of an Ohio farm.

Colonel Sir James Roberts, Surgeon to Lord Hardinge, the Viceroy, visited the leper asylum in company with his old college classmate, Colonel Hudson, the superintendent of the Naini Jail which is right next to the leper asylum. Sir James was much interested in the gardening which the lepers were doing. In order to give him more information, Colonel Hudson was kind enough to invite me to dinner one hot April evening. The dinner hour is eight. We sat on the lawn and talked until nearly three in the morning when Sir James said, ''When

Colonel Hudson was telling me about your agricultural work I thought you were just a missionary who had learned some new way of spending money, but I believe that you have got hold of something that can be of great help to India. If I could make arrangements for you, would you go to a number of the native states and give a few lectures in each one, telling of the possibilities for the improvement of agriculture in India, and how improved agriculture is at the very foundation of any improvement in the material prosperity of India; that it is out of India's fertile acres, properly cultivated, that must come the crops that can be sold to provide the money for food, clothing, schools, libraries, hospitals, museums, universities and all of the amenities of civilization?'' I said I would gladly go if I could be of any service. He arranged the trip. I spoke at Dhar, Dewas-Senior, Rutlam, Jaora, Indore. The lectures were usually given in the palace with the Maharajah as presiding officer, with the nobles of the state, and all his officials as audience. At Indore, the Hon. Mr. Tucker, Agent to the Governor-general, was the presiding officer. In each case the Maharajah had called in all his officers who understood English. I lectured and was much gratified at the great interest shown in agricultural things. Since that time a number of these states have put in their own departments of agriculture, most of which are doing excellent work. At the invitation of the late Maharajah, who was a young man not yet twenty years old and who had been at an English public school, I went to Jodhpur, where an audience of five thousand were gathered. There had been little rain for over a year and a half. The cattle were dying by the thousand and the people were at their wits' end. The Maharajah of Bikanir, one of India's representatives at the Peace Conference in Paris, a cultured gentleman, a great orator, a forward looking statesman, asked me to advise him in agricultural matters. I was invited to lecture in a number of other states but returned to America on a money raising campaign in 1914, returning to India in March, 1915.

When we got to Bombay letters were awaiting me from Dr. Janvier, the principal of the College, and from the officers of an Indian state government urging me to go immediately to the state to confer with the Maharajah. As soon as I had seen my wife and children safely settled in our bungalow at Allahabad I went over to this country where I found a very great interest aroused in agricultural improvement very largely through the conversation of Sir James Roberts with His Highness. The Maharajah sent me to stay in his guest house, an old palace, fitted up for the entertainment of his guests, and said to be the most beautiful guest house in India, certainly the most beautiful I have seen. He summoned me to the palace, jumped in his motor and took me and one of my colleagues along to a quiet little summer-house palace in a garden where he could be uninterrupted. For several hours he poured out to me his heart's desire for the improvement of the 3,000,000 of his subjects, only two per cent. of whom are literate, most of them poor and backward. The Maharajah is one of India's leading princes, and an exceedingly wise counselor. He has helped the British in many ways that have been made public and in a great many which the time has not yet come to disclose. He bought a great ocean liner and transformed it into a beautiful hospital-ship. Thousands of Indian and British wounded soldiers lift up hearts in gratitude to the Maharajah for the generous service rendered by this ship. He equipped and maintained a hospital in equatorial Africa. He sent all kinds of comforts to the troops. His own army, with equipment, was placed at the disposal of the British and maintained by him all during the war and was out of India for a good part of the war. His generosity was genuine and very far reaching. His example did a great deal to keep India loyal all through the dark days of the war. When the British government was very short of gold and silver coins the Maharajah let them have large amounts from his state treasury which helped to avert a financial panic. He is said to keep more small change on hand than any other person on earth.

The Maharajah is not only a generous ruler but exceedingly wise and sagacious and generally takes the long view. When he came to the throne his state was one of the most precarious, agriculturally, in the whole of India, and, because of the uncertain rainfall, more subject to famine than almost any other part of India. He called in the leading irrigation engineer of India then at the height of his fame. This engineer spent several years in working out an irrigation program which would protect the state in years when the rainfall was deficient or entirely lacking. This program is being carried out very successfully by an Indian engineer. This program has involved the building of enormous storage reservoirs and the laying of hundreds of miles of canals. The whole has cost approximately eleven million dollars and the end is not yet. The program is still going on. When this program is completed this state will then be the most secure of all the Indian states, instead of one of the most precarious. The main

line of the Great Indian Peninsular Railway passes
through this state. In addition there are two hundred
and seventy-five miles of two-foot-gauge feeder railway which has brought prosperity to districts formerly
inaccessible. About six hundred miles of the Grand
Trunk road from Bombay to Delhi is within this state
and is kept in first class condition by the state government. This stretch is one of the finest roads I have
ever motored over. In addition there are several hundred miles of excellent macadam feeder roads and His
Highness' program calls for much more. There is
nothing like a good road to bring prosperity to a backward territory. When the Maharajah's program is completed his state will be well protected and accessible.
With the splendid irrigation and transportation facilities, the next step naturally was the improvement of
agriculture. The Maharajah gave me his ideas and laid
down an outline of his plans. I was to fill in all details,
make a budget and check up and see that the scheme
was workable.

When the scheme was on paper and had been approved
by the Maharajah he asked me who was going to carry
it out. I told him that I considered the possibilities so
great that I thought he ought to go to the British government and get the very best agriculturist they had in
their service. There were seven hundred and fifty
thousand acres of land in his state which would have
been worth in the corn belt of America one hundred and
fifty to three hundred dollars per acre but not yielding
to him five cents per acre land revenue. It was worth
a good man to bring this under cultivation and populate
it with prosperous farmers. His Highness pointed out
that owing to the war, nearly every British officer that

could be spared had gone to the front and those that remained were carrying double burdens. Under the circumstances he said that it would not be fair to ask the British for an officer. Finally he said, "You have drawn up the scheme, why don't you carry it out?" I said there were serious objections as I was a Christian missionary and being a director of agriculture was hardly in line with my work. The Maharajah told me that he had cabled to our Missionary Board in New York asking them if they would allow me to act as Director of Agriculture for him and the answer he had received was, that if the mission, to which I belonged, and I personally were willing, the Board had no objection. Facing me with this he said, "Now your objections are removed, so resign from the mission and give your whole time to my state." I pointed out that owing to the war our Institute had also suffered, that we were short handed and heavily in debt and I had obligations to Allahabad that I could not possibly throw off on somebody else, so we finally agreed that one of my colleagues, an Agricultural Engineer, and I, as Director, were each to give eleven weeks each year of our time to work in the state. For this service the Maharajah paid the college over seven thousand dollars a year, none of which we touched personally. He then provided us with traveling expenses in the state and with a budget and equipment to do our work. In addition to an office staff I was given a motor and adequate tent equipage to travel over the state. The Agricultural Engineer was given funds for agriculture machinery, for a work-shop, show-room and an experimental laboratory for farm machinery. The budget sanctioned was most carefully drawn up and while not allowing for any extravagances was adequate to enable a most constructive piece of work to be done. The contract was signed for three years. It was recognized by both the Maharajah and the Mission that as a temporary war measure, such divided time was justified but as a permanency it would not be wise. The work to be done in the state called for a full time officer. In the three years I did my best to establish a department and get together a properly qualified staff, working smoothly. This was about all one could do with the interruptions and disappointments caused by the war, that prevented us getting out American helpers and American agricultural machinery. When I came home on furlough, August, 1919, one of my colleagues took over the job of officiating Director and another was put in charge of the second experimental and demonstration farm at the southern capital of the state.

The scheme finally approved by His Highness, called for, first, the building of a research laboratory; the laying out of an experimental and demonstration plot of about one hundred acres at the capital city. The equiping of the laboratory was done by one of my colleagues. Second, the building and equipping of an agricultural machinery show-room, work-shop, and experimental laboratory for farm machinery and thirdly, the establishment of demonstration villages over the state. The state is divided into eleven districts or counties each one having a county headquarters where the government offices, courts, police and treasuries are located. It was the Maharajah's idea that, at, or near, every county heaquarters a bankrupt village should be taken over by the Agricultural Department and transformed into a model demonstration village. Each village was to be in charge of an Indian who had had special training in agriculture and who was to make use of the village labor. It was to improve the condition of the poor farmers of the state that His Highness started the department; not to allow outsiders to come in to exploit it. Owing to the fact that there are such large areas of uncultivated land in the state, over six hundred thousand acres of excellent land lying idle, the Maharajah thought it best to get labor-saving machinery. About one million dollars was set aside for this purpose and orders were placed in America, but owing to the fact that the United States went into the war most of our orders were canceled and we received very little machinery. I recently heard from a firm of tractor builders in America that they have shipped this summer fourteen of the tractors to the Maharajah and I think before long the whole million dollars' worth of agricultural machinery will have been sent out. This is good business for the manufacturer and of very great value to India. Better farm tools and implements are at the very foundation of improved agriculture for India. With his present tools and implements the Indian farmer has gone as far as he can go. In case of failure of the rains or any other untoward circumstance he is compelled to sit in helpless inactivity. The ground is too hard for him to work. His little plow can not even scratch the hard ground. The American plow behind a tractor enables this hard ground to be properly opened up and broken down so that when the rain falls instead of most of the water running off, most of it soaks into the ground and, if the ground is then harrowed, is stored in the ground until the crops need it, just as in the case of our "dry farming" in the west of America. This deep plowing which turns under the manure and other organic matter that otherwise would be lost and which the soil of India needs so much, is very important. The agricultural engineer working in the Maharajah's agricultural experimental work-shop, devised a little plow made of steel. It is simple and cheap in construction; it can be easily repaired by the Indian blacksmith; it is of sufficiently light draft for the small under-nourished Indian oxen to draw it. This plow is one of the most useful inventions for India that has been devised within the last one hundred years. His idea was to work out a complete set of improved farm implements that will be within reach of the poor small farmer.

When the research laboratory and equipment were ready, through the kind offices of Mr. Bernard Coventry, formerly head of all government agricultural work in India, we were able to secure for the state the very valuable coöperation and advice of some of the best British Agricultural officers, notably Mr. and Mrs. Howard.

Three very busy years were spent in this state and when I left the program laid down by His Highness was still a long way from completion but the department was organized and a going concern. In addition to giving so much of my time in an official capacity to this state, I was called upon for advice which I was very glad to give, from other Indian rulers, notably Their Highnesses, the Maharajahs of Bikanir, Jodhpur, Benares, Alwar, Jamnagar. I was also advising the great Central Hindu University at Benares in their agricultural affairs and I felt in all this work a great opportunity to help India's poor and needy in a way that they could appreciate, in a language they could read and understand.

"And, behold, there came a leper and worshipped him, saying, Lord, if thou wilt, thou canst make me clean. And Jesus put forth his hand, and touched him saying, I will; be thou clean. And immediately his leprosy was cleansed." Math. 8: 2–3.

CHAPTER IX

THE MISSIONARY'S AVOCATION

During the Christmas vacation of 1903 I was sitting in a Mission prayer meeting in the Mission house at Katra at Allahabad. The missionaries were planning for and praying about their work. One of the older missionaries turned to me and said, "It is always the custom for the new man to have charge of the blind asylum and the leper asylum in addition to his regular work, so, Higginbottom, there is your job." He smiled and spoke with a great deal of confidence. If I had answered him on the spur of the moment it would have been without the smile, but no less confidence, and a flat contradiction. I did not think that caring for lepers was my job. I remembered my first Sunday evening in Calcutta, after having placed my goods in the hotel from the boat, I went out and stood on the corner of one of Calcutta's main thoroughfares and while I stood almost entranced by the wondrous surging tide of oriental life, to me so new and strange, passing before me, I was interrupted by hearing a thin, squeaky voice saying, "Bakhshish, Bakhshish, Sahib." I turned and close up to my face were a pair of stumps of hands. Instinctively I knew it was a leper. I had the idea that the greater the distance between us in the shortest possible time the better for me. I had not thought of lepers as belonging to

our modern world. I had heard of them in the Old
Testament days and in the time of our Lord. I thought
they were something that the world had outgrown. So
to be told that caring for these people was to be part
of my work was somewhat of a shock. As I sat there in
the prayer meeting and thought the thing through, I
had to admit that there were lepers in this modern day,
that leprosy was an awful disease, that being lepers they
were sick, and as sick needed somebody to care for them.
If somebody must care for them why not I be that
somebody? So before the prayer meeting was over I
said, "All right, if you think I am fit for that job I am
willing to tackle it."

I went to the blind asylum and saw fifty blind and
helpless cripples that were being cared for at the rate
of one dollar per month each. I looked after them for
four years but could do little for them. The blind
asylum has been turned over to the Mission. India has
a great many blind and no class of people in India is
having less done for them than these poor unfortunates.
There is urgent need that somebody or some organization take up their cause.

A few days after the prayer meeting Dr. Arthur H.
Ewing said to me, "Well, have you got your nerve with
you?" I said, "Yes, I think so, why?" He said,
"Well I think you will need it because we are going
over to the leper asylum." We jumped on our bicycles,
rode out of the college campus, across the Jumna bridge.
About a mile beyond the end of the bridge, upon that
sun-baked Indian plain, he pointed out a lot of ram-
shackle, tumble-down mud huts. He said, "That is the
leper asylum." As I caught my first view of it I
thought of all the unprepossessing institutions I had ever

seen that was surely the worst. It was only a few minutes until we were in the asylum and Dr. Ewing was
showing me around, introducing me to the inmates and
explaining my work to me.

What I saw on this first trip through the Leper Asylum was so awful and overwhelming that I had fully
made up my mind to tell Dr. Ewing that I did not feel
cut out for the job, that I considered the task would be
very much better done if he continued to do it rather
than turn it over to me. When I got back to the gate
I took hold of my bicycle and was taking what I thought
was my farewell look into that unlovely place, when I
happened to catch sight of an old man lying flat on his
back in the dust in the shadow of a tree. He had on
only a very small loin-cloth. You could see every rib.
His breath was coming with very great difficulty. What
were left of his hands and feet were all festered and
unbandaged and the flies were thick-clustered on the
open wounds. He was altogether the most loathsome
and repulsive human being I had ever seen. Yet as I
looked at him, it came over me that, after all, he was my
brother; in that unlovely, broken body there was a heart
that would respond to love and sympathy as would any
human heart, and more than all that, in that poor old
disease-rotted body there was a soul for which my Lord
had shed His blood, and who was I, that I should leave
him just because his need was so desperate? So I never
told Dr. Ewing that I would not care for the lepers. I
took hold of the job and found that the asylum was
supported by the Allahabad Charitable Association, an
organization trying to do a great work on entirely insufficient funds. It was responsible for the blind, and
the cripples in their asylum, for a number of indigent

Indian Christian widows, for a number of poor European and Anglo-Indians; altogether too much for its meagre income. The result was that the lepers were living in houses not fit for human habitation with insufficient food and clothing. Everything the leper got had to come out of one dollar a month for each leper, food, clothing, medicines and attendance. The result was that if any leper had feet enough left to walk on and strength enough to walk he considered that he could do so much better begging than he could in the asylum that he went out to beg in the Bazaar. I decided that, in the condition it was, the institution had no right to exist. It should either be mended or ended.

There is an organization that is known as the Mission to Lepers, founded in 1874 by a missionary to India, Mr. Wellesley C. Bailey. The operations of this mission have gradually extended until now it has charge of asylums in every continent, about eighty in all. The Mission to Lepers came along and said to the Charitable Association, "Turn the asylum over to us and we will be entirely responsible for it and spend more money than you are able to. We will also rebuild and give habitable quarters to the lepers." The transfer was made and the Mission to Lepers asked the Presbyterian Mission if I might continue as Superintendent. The Mission gave its consent. The Mission to Lepers asked me what my plans were. I went to study the best asylums in India, got a number of ideas from each one and laid out a scheme for the rebuilding and management of the asylum. As these asylums are all voluntary it is essential that the management be such as to make the asylum more attractive to the leper than begging or wandering about the country. The leper can not be treated as a criminal and be put on prison diet. The lepers so often have said to me, "Sahib, we are not criminals, we are only unfortunate." The food for a leper, who is a sick man, must be better than the food for the prisoner in jail. When the Mission to Lepers took over the asylum we started our building program and immediately displaced the miserable old mud huts with brick and mortar structures having good roofs with iron battens instead of bamboos, and good French pattern tile instead of the small country tile. The hospital was built with two wards for men and one for women and a dispensary properly equipped, a store room, two large tanks in the asylum for the washermen to wash the clothing. Heretofore the washermen had taken the lepers' clothing down to the river to the regular "Dhobi Ghat" where all the city clothing is washed, much to the danger of the general public. When the lepers were comfortably housed and the hospital built and running, we next secured, about a mile away, a home for the un-tainted children of the lepers where the children could be kept apart from their parents, trained, educated and given their chance in life. An Indian widow gave the site. After this the next building to be built was the church and instead of having beautiful, stained-glass windows we have great big arches with chicken-wire screens. This is to make certain that the ventilation is good. My wife and I like to be present for the Sunday morning services. With a congregation of from three to five hundred lepers, unless the ventilation is good, one is apt to be in distress.

The Mission to Lepers placed at my disposal twenty-five dollars a year for each adult leper and twenty dollars for each child. Out of that, all food, clothing, medi-

cines, servants, had to be provided. Even with the en-
larged sum of two dollars per month for each leper, I
had my troubles in keeping the lepers reasonably well
fed, and decently clothed with proper medicine and service. So many of the lepers have lost all their fingers,
sometimes the whole hand clear back to the wrist, that
it is obviously impossible for such a man to do his own
cooking, so I get some other leper to do the cooking for
this one and pay the cook about seven cents a month
for his extra work. Each man gets four yards of cotton cloth, forty inches wide, which costs about sixty
cents, a year for clothing. This is his morning suit, his
afternoon suit, if he has any evening engagements, it
is his glad rags, when he goes to bed at night it is his
bed sheet. Among the lepers of India it costs more to
correctly gown a lady than it does to clothe a gentleman, for, in northern India, in order to conform to social
custom a woman must have her head covered. So instead
of four yards of cotton cloth it takes six yards for her.
This she winds around, making a skirt of it, then brings
it up over one shoulder and under the opposite armpit,
making a shirtwaist out of it, and then it goes up over
the head making the "Chaddar" or head covering.
With this one piece of cloth so arranged she is dressed,
ready to go anywhere. With so little clothing it is very
difficult for the men and women to keep clean and I am
therefore deeply grateful to the many friends in Scot-
land, the United States, Canada, Australia and New
Zealand who have at various times sent us bundles of
shirts for the men and middy blouses for the women,
and mufflers and socks for both. These we give out at
Christmas and always feel sorry that we don't have
enough to go round. Several times my wife and I have

been threatened to be mobbed by the disappointed ones who failed to receive a garment at the Christmas treat. A blanket which now costs about two dollars is issued every second year. Medicines and bandages will average about thirty cents a month for each leper. The wages of the doctor, the compounder and hospital assistants, servants, washermen and the sweepers or scavengers use up most of the rest of the money. I used to issue all food to the lepers. I soon learned that I knew so little about Indian food and what the people liked that I was in constant trouble. After talking it over with the lepers, it was decided to give each leper about a pound of grain a day. Some prefer wheat, some rice, some millet and some a mixture of barley and peas. Whatever they preferred, they had. At their request I built in the asylum a little country store and one of the lepers was put in charge as storekeeper. In this store was kept the many different kinds of pulse, spices, curries and condiments that make Indian food so wondrously tasteful and so marvelously indigestible. After having provided clothing, medicines, servants and the grain ration, it worked out that there was about eight cents a week left for each leper to spend at the store. This was given to him on Saturday morning and he could spend it in any way he liked—buying any luxuries that his fancy dictated and that could be bought at the rate of one cent per day. It was one of the social events of the day for the leper to go and do his shopping. One cent in North India does not buy any more than one cent in North America but Indian merchants are in the habit of selling smaller amounts of commodities. The anna, value two American cents, breaks up into twelve "pies" so that with one American cent a person could buy six different things.   Of course it was only a half-teaspoonful of sugar, a soup-spoonful of salt, a head of garlic, a few red peppers or other spices.   The amount of ghee or clarified butter that they could buy for one-sixth of a cent was so small, I often thought that if any of them should have been so unfortunate as to lose it he would have to borrow a magnifying glass to find it again.   Before any money leaves the Asylum to go out into circulation it is carefully sterilized.

In the early days when I went over to the leper asylum I would be surrounded by a lot of the lepers, fighting, wrangling and squabbling, asking me to decide between them.   They would complain that some one had stolen their food or their clothing or their cooking utensils. I am sure that if I had as little of these as the lepers had, I should not have felt very badly at acquiring a little more, even at the expense of my neighbors.   I had a great deal of sympathy for the thief, but I had a little more for the man or woman who had lost his dinner, and what is more, I had to provide him with a new one which often put me into serious difficulty.   As I studied this quarrelsomeness among the lepers I found that most of it was due to the fact that there were twenty-four hours in every day and the leper had nothing to do but think about himself and his own trouble.   He was bound to be into mischief of one sort or another.   The leper is the greatest traveler in India.   He is constantly going from one shrine or holy place to another, from one "Mahatma," a man claiming to be divine, an incarnation of one of the gods, and, if divine, able to heal all manner of sickness and disease, to another.   I have seen one of these Mahatmas sitting on the banks of the Ganges clothed in the four directions, that being sufficient clothing for a god, having wrapped up in a dirty little towel, correspondence with women, society leaders, in some of our American cities whom he had known when lecturing as a Swami to American audiences. He was telling our students what fools they were to let missionaries teach them the Bible, as it was not taught in America any more. I do not blame the leper for traveling so much, since his quest is in search of health, but it made my work among the lepers very difficult. It seemed as if I were running some sort of a transient hotel where the lepers could come in for a day or two, pull themselves together and out again. In those early days at least ninety-five per cent. of the lepers in the asylum on the first of January were off again on their travels before the thirty-first of December. I conceived that the duty of a superintendent of a leper asylum is two-fold. First, he is to care for the leper, and obey Jesus' command to cleanse the leper. Secondly, he is to protect the public from the menace of the leper at large.

After studying a number of occupations, recognizing the physical limitations of the leper, realizing that nothing made in the leper asylum could be sold outside, but must be consumed in the asylum, and having seen the wonderful results of Colonel Hudson's garden in the jail I decided that we would have gardening in the leper asylum. When I announced this to the lepers they said, "But that is work, is it not, Sahib?" I said, "Yes, it can be so considered." They said, "If it is work we don't want anything to do with it." I had to bribe them to take to the work. I gave seeds of fruit, vegetables and flowers to as many as I could persuade to take them. I offered prizes beginning with five rupees, four, three, two, one, down to two annas. With nine months practically rainless every year it is necessary to provide some irrigation. The government very kindly bored deeper the well which gave us an unfailing supply of water. The well cylinder was ninety feet deep and boring was continued another seventy-five feet, a four inch tube sunk, when we struck an underground stream of water. The usual method of raising water from wells in India is by means of oxen and a big bucket, a long rope, and a pulley wheel set on pillars over the mouth of the well. I followed the custom of the country and bought my first pair of oxen. I paid fifteen dollars for them. I felt quite proud of my bargain. To think of actually buying two live oxen, each one having a head, tail and four legs, for fifteen dollars seemed a great bargain. After these oxen had been at work for some time I made a very interesting discovery. I learned that this pair of oxen could not draw enough water out of that well, to irrigate enough ground, to grow enough food to feed themselves, let alone irrigate enough ground to grow enough food for the lepers. I solved this problem by cabling Montgomery-Ward and getting out a steam boiler and engine, bought a pump, and then the lepers had an abundant supply of good water; gardening was possible. The first prize that year was won by a woman. I never saw her stand up. She literally had nothing to stand on, but crawling out on her hands and knees with a short length of barrel hoop she played and worked and loved around her little plot until she had a beautiful and productive garden. When the lepers learned that whatever they grew they could have for themselves, that I did not take it from them, gardening became more popular. Their fear had been that I was going to get them to grow the stuff and then take it away from them.   We planted out a lot of mango, guava, orange, and lemon trees, papitas and bananas.   Imagine I have given a man or woman a banana shoot about eighteen inches high.   He plants it and waters it and in that rich soil and sunshine it is soon up ten to twelve feet. The big heart-shaped purple flower appears like the knob of a shepherd's crook and as each petal falls off, out shoots a little green finger-like banana.   It is not very long until there is a great big beautiful bunch of bananas.   About the time it is ripening I notice a little wooden bed at the foot of the banana plant and I say to the man or woman on it, "Hello, have you taken to living the simple life, do you find that sleeping in the open air improves your complexion?"   "O, no, Sahib, it is not that but that my friends and neighbors have become so interested in this bunch of bananas that they are sampling them and if I want any for myself I must stay pretty close by."   Or imagine a man with a cauliflower patch or potatoes just about ready.   It does not matter what a priest or Mahatma a thousand miles away says about curing leprosy, the man with the garden patch says, "I planted it and watered it and before I leave I am going to taste the fruit thereof."   So with the good hand of our God upon us, gardening has been a great blessing to the asylum.   It has given the leper something to occupy his time, something more to eat, has made discipline easy and has been of the greatest service in keeping the leper in the asylum.   Ninety-eight per cent. of the lepers in the asylum have come to regard it as their permanent home.   They do not wander, they do not want to be driven out as they have established themselves in their little houses and are as happy as people can be suffering from such a terrible disease.

When the church was about finished a number of the lepers came to me and said, "Whose church is this?" I said, "Well, the ladies in Ireland who sent out the money to build it, said it was to be for lepers, so as far as any church can belong to man it is yours." They said, "Well, if it is our church we would like to have some part in it." I said, "Well, I don't see what you can do, you have no money." They said, "But, Sahib, have we not been praying for this church for years, and if we were praying don't you think we were saving up?" I said, "Well, you get so little that I don't see what you could save out of." They said, "Well, we have saved and we have got money and we would like to have some part in the church." So they bought the pulpit Bible, the largest the Bible Society puts out in the Hindu language. They also bought a clock and a bell so that they could be prompt in their attendance at service. They give regularly to all the Presbyterian causes. They give to the Bible and Tract Society. During the war they took up two collections a year for comforts for the wounded Indian soldiers, giving in some collections over thirty dollars. I can not go before this leper asylum congregation and tell them of any worthy cause or needy individual but what they say, "Can we not help?" I feel that if there is any person on earth that I could forgive, and forgive gladly, for being selfish and self-centered it is the leper. When one thinks of the misery and the pain of the disease and the mental attitude induced by the suffering, I would not blame the leper for saying, "I get so little that all I get I want for myself," and yet I have known leper men and women, when something appealed to them, to put the whole eight cents into the collection plate at once, denying themselves the pleasure of going to the little country store to do their shopping; living a whole week on bread made without raising of any kind, just meal and water mixed together, in order that their eight cents might go to the spreading of Christ's gospel. To these lepers Christ seems so real, His treatment so practical, that there is an intimacy in the way they speak of Him that shows a depth of faith seldom found.

Fifteen years ago in the American Mission Famine Orphanage at Lalitpur was a girl of seventeen, Frances by name, sweet, attractive, a general favorite, engaged to be married, one of the most capable girls in the institution. There came on her hands, round the joints of her fingers, some sores that refused to heal in spite of the application of every remedy the lady missionaries possessed. An English physician was called in who said the girl was suffering from leprosy and should be removed at once from the orphanage. The lady superintendent wrote to me to ask if the girl could be admitted to the Naini Leper Asylum. I wrote back asking her to send the girl. A few days later while I was seated at breakfast, the arrival of callers was announced. It proved to be Frances and her brother, who had just been graduated from the Methodist Episcopal Theological Seminary at Bareilly. I told them to drive on over to the Asylum and I would catch up with them on my bicycle. After finishing my breakfast I rode over and caught up with them just before reaching the Asylum. We walked in together. It was not into the new asylum with its fine buildings and well laid out and flourishing gardens, but into that old unspeakable place. Leprosy so often makes me think of strong drink. It is bad enough when it gets control of a man, but infinitely worse when it gets control of a woman. What the leper women looked like in the early days when I first took charge of the asylum is hard to describe. They were so dirty, so careless of their personal appearance, their faces so hopeless that it did not seem right to call them women, and one strove in vain for a word that adequately described them. Frances, dressed in her beautiful, white flowing garments as for some gala occasion, walked with her brother and me into that awful place. She caught sight of some of those creatures who sat gossiping under the shade of the neem trees. Frances took one look, then she threw her head on her brother's shoulder and sobbed as though her heart would break. "My God," she cried, "am I going to become as they are? Is that what is in store for me?" Her brother had to go back to his work and I had to go back to mine and we must leave her in the Leper Asylum. Frances was so distressed that I was afraid she might attempt to destroy herself so I asked several of the old men to guard the well and see she did not get into it. A few days later my wife and I were over at the Asylum. I said to Frances, "I deeply sympathize with you, I know words are poor things to express what I feel for you in this awful affliction. Yet in spite of it all, is this not true? In that orphanage those American women brought certain things into your life that have made it richer and fuller and better than the lives of the other women in the asylum?" She assented. I then continued, "How would it be for you to try to bring some of those things out of your richer life and put them into the lives of these other leper women and children?" She promised to try. My wife fitted her out with supplies. She started a little school. She taught the women to sing, the children to read and write. She had learned to play the piano in the orphanage. So I got a friend to buy for her a little folding organ. This was a great joy to her and helped her in her work. Gradually there came a transformation over the women's quarters. The houses were made clean and neat and tidy. The women also improved in appearance. They washed their clothes, combed their hair, and tried to make themselves attractive. When the very hot weather came, my wife had to take our little baby daughter up to the mountains. I went to our Women's Hospital and said to the lady in charge, "Dr. Binford, the leper women do so miss the visits of my wife, if you would go over to the Asylum some afternoon you would cheer them greatly. They are very grateful for the visits of an American woman." She promised to go and a few days later with Miss Alice Wishart and another lady missionary she drove over. On their way back they drove through the college campus where we were playing tennis. After our game I strolled over to their phaeton. Dr. Binford said, " Mr. Higginbottom, Frances opened her heart to me to-day. She said that when she first went into the asylum she could not believe that there was a God, or if there were a God, she did not see how He could be a God of love and afflict any one as He had afflicted her, but Frances went on to say that now she could see it all. God had a work for her to do, ministering to the other lepers. If she had not herself become a leper she would never have discovered her work, so she said every day I live now I thank Him for having sent me here and given me this work to do."

For fifteen years I have known Frances. I have seen her work. I know that greater than anything she says is the witness of her own life. That first heartbreaking aid toward the maintenance, so that to-day the government practically covers every dollar of mission money with one dollar of government funds. As no money is spent for the salaries of superintendents (they all give their services and are supported by their respective missions) it is easy to see that a great deal can be accomplished in caring for the lepers for a small investment of money. The leper that sat by the roadside and, as Jesus passed by, said unto Him, "Lord, if Thou wilt Thou canst make me clean," is often in my mind. The record tells us that Jesus stretched forth His hand and said, "I will, be thou clean," and immediately his leprosy was cleansed. The leper had been thrust outside the camp, was outside the pale of human society, and Jesus by that touch brought him back into the human family. And I take it that the work of the Mission to Lepers is conceived in the spirit that Jesus showed, of bringing this poor unfortunate, that man despises, back into the human family.

"Replenish the earth, and subdue it."   Gen. 1: 28.

"Ye shall know the truth and the truth shall make you free."
John 8: 32.

"Gather up the fragments that remain that nothing be lost."
John 6: 12.

CHAPTER X

JESUS' EXAMPLE FOR SUCH WORK

I went out to India having specialized in philosophy and hoping to be an evangelist. I end up by being a missionary farmer. I have had friends tell me they could not see why I am interested in the things in which I am interested. They ask what plows, harrows, tractors, silos, threshing machines, and better cattle have to do with the evangelization of India. Bulletins upon the use of manure and silage are good, but what is their value as missionary tracts?

I am accused of having lost my first love and of having grown cold, of having become a materialist, and of having lost my aspirations, of being indifferent to spiritual and eternal things, of caring only for the things of time and sense, the things that shall pass away, that are not eternal. Now I cannot be indifferent to such criticism from such sources. I do not doubt the honesty and kindliness of my critics. It behooves me therefore to see what there is in such criticism. For, if it is true and justified, my work is a hindrance rather than a help to the spread of Christ's kingdom in India. I should deeply deplore such a result.

In speaking of this criticism I do not wish to give the impression that the whole missionary body is opposed to this kind of work. In fact there is a very large majority who heartily approve and wish it God speed.

124

Again and again when insurmountable obstacles seemed
to block the way these friends, in every way possible,
have helped to overcome the difficulties and encouraged
the Agricultural Institute to persevere.   They have said
that if in Christian literate America, with its abundant
wealth and widespread education, there is need for
Hampton, Mount Hermon, Tuskeegee, Berea, Kentucky,
and the Rockefeller Foundation; how much more in
poor, illiterate, non-Christian India.   I wish therefore
to express my hearty and grateful thanks to all those,
both in India and America, who are helping to make the
Agricultural Institute an effective instrument for helping India to help itself.   The following quotations from
the minutes of the National Missionary Council of India
show how the representatives, both Indian and foreign, of
all the evangelical missions in India regard such work.

From Proceedings of the Fourth Meeting of the National Missionary Council, Coonoor, November 9–13,
1917.

Resolved:

XX–1. The Council endorses the view that Agricultural and Industrial Missions are an integral part of the
presentation of the Gospel to India at this time.

From Proceedings of the Fifth Meeting of the National Missionary Council, Benares, November 14–19,
1918.

Resolved:

XII-1.   That in the opinion of the council missions
should aim at the establishment of central institutions
for the training of teachers in agriculture and allied industries in the various language or climatic areas.

2. That as far as possible teachers thus trained should
be employed.

3. That the Council recommends missions in mass movement areas to definitely plan for adequate instruction in agriculture and allied industries, such as silk, poultry, the making and repairing of agricultural tools and implements.

4. That the Council urges upon the Home Boards the necessity of providing an adequate supply of trained men and suitable equipment to carry on agricultural and allied industrial training, especially in mass movement areas.

I realize that I am living this life only once, that if I make a mistake with it, there is no chance to come back again and do the thing right. I understand that the Will of God is the supreme thing for my life, the only thing that really matters. It is not whether I am a missionary that matters, or not a missionary, but wherever I live and whatever I do, God's Will is first, the controlling factor that determines the whole of my life. Further, I am not afraid of His Will. Trying to obey it has led me to do some things I would not have done on my own initiative. But I have always found that His Will has been infinitely larger and better than my own will for my life. When choosing my own course for myself I have made so many mistakes, missed the way so often, that I gladly turn over the guidance of my life to His Will and trust it fully. Should I for any reason whatsoever fail to do His Will with my life, I should consider that the greatest possible tragedy. I am anxious to do His Will as soon as I see it. There is often great difficulty to know what His Will is.

I have found His Will for my life most clearly laid

down in the Bible. I consider the Bible the one up-to-date book in a world where most books are soon out of date and behind the times and needs of men. When a boy on my father's farm in Wales it was reading the Bible hours each day by myself for over a year, fighting it all the time, that caused me to offer Him my life without condition or reservation. I sought to know His Will for my life and I was not sure that I knew what it was. I knew His last command to His disciples was to go into all the world, to preach the Gospel, to teach all nations, teaching them to observe all things whatsoever He had commanded. I was not sure where He wanted me, or what He wanted me to do. But until He made the way plain, I considered it was my duty to get ready to obey His last command and prepare for that which was farthest off, and if He wanted me anywhere else it would be easy for Him to stop me at any intermediate place, if that were where He wanted me to live my life and do my work.

So when criticisms became severe and I felt uncertain of myself it was again to this Book that I went. I wanted to be sure first of all that I knew what the Gospel, the "Good News," really was. I studied anew the life of Our Lord. I noticed that on the threshold of His public ministry He went into the synagogue where He had been brought up and, as was His custom, the village carpenter stood up to read. The scroll was handed to Him and He unwound it till He found the place where it is written, "The Spirit of the Lord is upon me, because He hath anointed me to preach the Gospel to the poor, He hath sent me to heal the broken-hearted, to preach deliverance to the captives, and recovering of the sight to the blind, to set at liberty those that are bruised, to preach the acceptable year of the Lord.'' St. Luke 4:16 et al.

The first thing I notice is that the Spirit was upon Jesus for service. ''To preach the Gospel to the poor.'' That I take to mean the oral, the spoken, presentation of His truth about salvation. A great many good people would stop with this oral presentation of the Gospel because they are afraid of works. It is true that Jesus placed preaching first, but it is only part of His message. He continued, ''He hath sent me to heal the broken-hearted, to preach deliverance to the captives and recovering of sight to the blind, to set at liberty them that are bruised.'' Jesus' Gospel is preaching plus action which explains and gives content to the preaching. We can take all of these clauses in their primary literal sense, and from the literal interpretation find a place for helping India's outcaste, broken-hearted and broken-spirited by centuries of persecution, degradation and oppression, we can find warrant for medical missions and all other forms of humanitarian and social service. We can take all of these clauses in their spiritual and figurative sense and some would say, their fuller sense, and find out that Christ was anointed to help all human life, to make it better, to rid it of wrong and oppression. In other words His complete Gospel is more than an oral presentation, more than a matter of words. It calls for doing as well as being, the act that proves the faith, ''Not every one that saith unto me, Lord, Lord, but he that doeth my Will''; ''He that heareth my words and doeth shall be likened unto a wise man.'' ''If any man will do His Will, he shall know of the doctrine.''

The object of the Gospel is to save mankind. It is to help men whenever or wherever they need help, for the present time as well as for eternity. Instead of despising this body and this present life God thought so much of these that He gave His only begotten Son a human body and He shared our life with all its limitations. And in this human flesh dwelt very God of very God, the Lamb slain from before the foundation of the world. If man in his present state be not the object of the Gospel, what purpose does it have? "He that believeth hath (present tense) eternal life," now. When God through Christ saves a person, eternal life for that person has already begun. Death makes only a change in place and state. The individual persists.

This statement from Isaiah which He read in the synagogue where every one knew Him can be taken as the program for His own life. "This day is this scripture fulfilled in your ears." If we read on to the end of the chapter we have a very complete demonstration of how He Himself carried out His own program. "Now when the sun was setting, all they that had any sick with divers diseases brought them unto Him; and He laid His hands on every one of them and healed them." To one who has lived in an oriental country this picture is a very full one. Disease is so common, so much of it is incurable, human life slips away so easily; remedies that cure are so few. The watchers sitting by the loved one, who is tossing in fever, writhing in pain, are unable to help, dreading the night when life goes out all too effortless. At the hour of greatest dread and terror He laid His hand on every one of them, and healed them. There is no incurable ward in Jesus' hospital, no long, lingering, tedious convalescence, He healed them all. Another striking demonstration is recorded in St. Matthew 9:35. And this healing of the body is part of His Gospel.

His first miracle confirms His program for His own life. There is great significance in this first miracle of Christ at the wedding at Cana, the turning of water into wine. The occasion, the place, the fact that it was His first miracle and that the miracle was what it was, should be noted. He knew how His every act would be scrutinized. With Him there was no forgetting the import of what He did, no waste movement, no slip, no second try, no failure to take into account the vista of history. His first miracle was so chosen by Him as to reveal His meaning to the world, it is full of purpose. By His first miracle He turned water into wine. In these days there are many who are afraid of this miracle. They think it would have been better had he turned wine into water. He actually turned water into wine; He gave color to that which had no color; He gave taste to the tasteless; He gave sweetness to that which lacked sweetness; He gave brightness and sparkle where it had not before existed; He satisfied man's taste. He completely changed the water into wine, something totally different, He enriched water into wine. Surely He comes into our dull, drab colorless lives and enriches them in a way that is beyond the power of any person to explain. No, the greatest miracle of all is the way He comes into human life so that it is not what it was before He came. So great is the change which He makes when He comes into our lives that we call it a "new birth"; and it is nothing less.

We have seen what Jesus considered the program for His own life work. We have noted how He carried out

His program. In St. Matthew 10 : 7–8 in sending forth
the twelve He lays down a program for His disciples.
"As ye go, preach, saying, The Kingdom of Heaven is at
hand. Heal the sick, cleanse the leper, raise the dead,
cast out devils, freely ye have received freely give."

Again it is evident that while He puts preaching first it
is not all of His Gospel. A series of coördinate clauses
give the other parts of His Gospel. "Heal the sick, etc."
So many people tell me they are interested in the work
God has given me to do because, like medical missions,
"it is a good wedge for the Gospel." When people say
this, I wonder what their conception of the Gospel is. Is
it sermons only, statements of doctrine, words arranged
in tomes of theology, words of fire to convict of sin,
words of forgiveness to him who repents, words of hope
to cheer the pilgrim on his way, words to comfort the
mourner? All these it surely is and must be, but all
this does not fill out the compass of His Gospel, nor test
its fullest length or depth, breadth or height.

I utterly repudiate the "wedge theory" for the Gospel. The Gospel that I received of the Lord Jesus needs
no wedge. A Gospel that needs a wedge needs careful
examination. It is not the Gospel that Jesus brought
into the world. If the Gospel is not its own wedge then
it is the most colossal and pathetic failure of history.
Medical missions are the Gospel. Cleansing the lepers
is the Gospel, as much as preaching is the Gospel. These
carry out His specific commands as much as preaching
does. Is not the slow progress of the Gospel over the
world to-day partly due to the fact that believers have
often had a one-sided and incomplete Gospel? Less than
Jesus laid down as the Gospel? People can often better
understand the oral presentation, if there has been loving

service to give content to the words, to prove that the
words have Life back of them. The word became flesh.
Jesus' matchless sermons and parables are strengthened
by His deeds. When challenged it was not to His words
but to His works He appealed, "Many good works have
I shewed you from my Father; for which of those works
do ye stone me?" St. John 10: 32.

Again when John the Baptist was in prison, doubts
arose in his mind as to whether Jesus was really the
One that should come. He sent two of his disciples to
ask Jesus, "And in that same hour He cured many of
their infirmities and plagues, and of evil spirits; and unto
many that were blind He gave sight. Then Jesus an-
swering said unto them, Go your way and tell John what
things ye have seen and heard, how that the blind see,
the lame walk, the lepers are cleansed, the deaf hear, the
dead are raised, to the poor the Gospel is preached."

This He offers as proof of His Messiahship, and in this
instance He does not mention preaching till the last; His
healing of the body and caring for its needs come first
into His mind in this hour when He wants to strengthen
the faith of him of whom He says that of those born of
women there is not a greater prophet than John the
Baptist.

There is a very real danger that all desire to guard
against. The danger is in substituting "service" for
"salvation," business for Godliness. We are commanded
to "work out" our own salvation, something we already
possess, not to work in order to gain salvation. The idea
that work, if there is only enough of it, can save a sinner
from his sins is held by some. I was asked to give an
address to a company of students to answer the question

"Is not such work as yours capable of being carried on without the religious, Christian motive?" "Can not a person who does not believe in Jesus Christ as the world's only Saviour do such work?" I had to answer that I was a poor one of whom to ask such a question for I had never tried to do my work apart from religion. My work I take to be the expression of the fact that I believe God. I had always done it believing that it was God's Will for me and I could do nothing else. I am satisfied that the religious motive must be present, that Jesus is the only one who can supply the continuing power to carry on through all circumstances and all the time.

As followers of Him we can do what He has commanded us to do giving Him His rightful place in it, as the Author and Finisher not only of our faith, but of our work also, which is but the expression of that faith. Many are afraid of the "Social Gospel" as they call it, because it brings them so near the world, because they fear the complications that are likely to arise, that they will do more than the Gospel really calls for. There is a real danger in this, but I think we must risk it. Far better to go two miles with Him than one. There are those also who are opposed to the "Social Gospel" out of sheer laziness. It would break up the regularity of their comfortable, ordered lives. To provide material requisites to feed the hungry would rob them of time for contemplation.

There are thirty-six miracles recorded in the four Gospels. Twenty-eight tell of healing disease, raising to life, giving sight to the blind, feeding the hungry, casting out demons. Eight do not have this personal intimate relation to some individual or group in need. The great majority have to do with meeting immediate human need.

Why did Jesus perform these miracles? Some say to teach spiritual lessons, to give preachers texts for sermons wherefrom they can draw analogies between the physical ill and the spiritual ill. I have no objection to any one getting all the spiritual meaning he can out of the miracles of Jesus. I think it well, however, to remember that the primary object of Jesus in performing these miracles was to meet the present physical needs of those He healed or fed as well as to forgive their sins.

I never go into the leper asylum of which I have charge without thinking of that leper who, as Jesus passed by said, "Lord, if thou wilt Thou canst make me clean." Jesus said, "I will," and put forth His hand and touched him saying, "I will, be thou clean." And immediately his leprosy was cleansed. That fair, pure hand of the Son of God touched that disease-rotted body and it was clean. This man who had been outside the pale of ordinary society, by that touch, was brought back into the human family. Why did Jesus cleanse the leper? To enable men to draw analogies between leprosy and sin? Or was it, that seeing the desperate need of the leper and the leper's faith, He healed him? Jesus healed the leper because he was a leper and it was from leprosy he needed relief. It was his physical need and Jesus' ability to meet that need that caused Him to heal the leper.

The blind man found out that Jesus was passing by. He had faith to believe Jesus could give him sight and Jesus spat upon his eyes and the man saw. It was the man's blindness that moved the Great Heart with compassion and He healed him.

I think of the five thousand far from home, out in the desert, hungry, tired, night coming down. Jesus commanded His disciples to feed the multitude. They showed how impossible His command was, again He insisted "Give ye them to eat." They found the boy with the loaves and fishes, all they had. They brought it all to Jesus. Jesus took the five loaves and two fishes and blessed and brake and not only were all fed and had all they would eat, but there were twelve baskets full more than were required. These twelve baskets were not the leavings, the offal, but were there ready to be distributed to any who needed more. God's measure is always abundant, no niggardly hand when He is Provider, He prepares more than we need.

Jesus fed this great multitude because they were hungry, physically. It was their need that appealed to Him. He drew no spiritual lesson at this time. The next day He preached His sermon and emphasized that He is the Bread of Life. "I am the Living Bread, if any man shall eat of this bread he shall live forever." Nowhere else does He make greater claims for Himself than in this sermon that came as a result of feeding the multitude. Before He preached the sermon He fed the crowd. Would not the church be wise to copy her Lord in this wherever necessary? As He looks out over stricken Armenia; over famine cursed China; over a large part of Europe where the children to-day are dying of hunger; over India where from the cradle to the grave a multitude, over one hundred millions, are chronically hungry, does he say less to His disciples to-day in

America than He said that day in Galilee? I think not.
If we bring to Him all we have and let Him bless it and
break it, we will see the continuing miracle. We ourselves will have all we need and the hungry everywhere
will be fed. His command still holds to feed the physical hunger, and after that the spiritual hunger with the
Bread of Life that came down from heaven and giveth
life to the world. He came that they might have life and
have it more abundantly.

I think again of that great picture drawn for us in the
twenty-fifth chapter of St. Matthew's Gospel. The nations are separated from one another as a shepherd separates the sheep from the goats. The sheep on His right
hand, the goats on His left. To those on His right hand
He says, "Come ye blessed of my Father, inherit the
kingdom prepared for you from the foundation of the
world." It is significant that no commendation is given
to those who have not gone to their needy fellows and
helped them where their need was. They say unto Him,
"Why, Lord, for what do you call us blessed? What have
we ever done?" And Jesus says, "You saw me hungry
and ye gave me to eat." They say, "Hold on there
Lord, are you not going too fast, making some mistake?
We never saw you, let alone saw you hungry." "O, yes
you did," Jesus says. "When you went to that little
famine-cursed Indian village that had been growing ten
bushels of wheat per acre and you taught it to grow
twenty you were helping to feed the hungry." "When
you went to that village that was growing sixty pounds
of poor short-staple cotton per acre and taught them to
grow three hundred pounds per acre of good long-staple
cotton you were helping to clothe the naked." "When

you went to that village where the well had dried up and you sent a boring outfit, and bored down until you had secured an abundant supply of water, enough for man and beast and some over for irrigation, you were helping to give drink to the thirsty.'' ''When the doctor opened his hospital for the poor and lowly who otherwise would have no medical aid, he was visiting the sick.'' ''When you go to India's outcastes, to her 'untouchables' whom man despiseth, who have suffered age-long, untellable wrongs in the fearful prison of caste, and freed them from its bondage and caused them to walk as free men, that was done unto Me.'' ''Lord, we never thought of You there or in that degraded state.'' ''O, yes, take the veil from that little humble Indian village outcaste, I am there. Inasmuch as ye did it to the lowest and meanest of India's outcastes ye did it unto Me.''

This is the great glory of Christ's Gospel. It is the one full, complete program, adequate for man's needs for time and eternity. It comes to man in his neediest hour and sets his feet upon a rock and puts a new song in his mouth. The Gospel is the only sufficient program for the individual. The nations have tried everything else but the Gospel and they have failed to learn how to avoid war and get peace, why not give the Gospel a chance in national life as well as in individual life? I believe the golden rule in national life will bring greater victories than armies and navies. The nations still believe in armies and navies after the collapse of military Germany who said, ''Given guns enough, what need of God?'' America's Secretary of the Navy wants to make her navy the greatest in the world. Does history record that an army or navy ever really saved a nation whose sole trust was in the power of heavy artillery or battle-ship? It is the rightness, the justness of the cause that nerves men's wills, that teaches them how to fight.

To sum up we see that Christ's program for His own life, the carrying out of that program in practical demonstration in His miracles, His commands to His disciples, His commendation of those who feed the hungry, clothe the naked, give drink to the thirsty, all call for more than preaching. They call for the practical application of that which gives a meaning and content to the oral presentation of God's truth. I believe the church would do well to pay more attention rather than less to this aspect of the Gospel. Many who cannot understand or interpret words, can understand loving deeds. I am not decrying preaching. We need more of it not less, we need The Word become flesh. Preaching is one of the most powerful forces in the world to-day. Knox, Calvin, Wesley, Spurgeon, Moody, have made history.

The place in the missionary program of the work we are trying to do at Allahabad falls in with events as recorded in the sixth chapter of Acts. There had been a great ingathering "The number of the disciples was multiplied, there arose a murmuring of the Grecians against the Hebrews because their widows were neglected in the daily ministrations." Then the twelve called the multitude of disciples unto them and said, "It is not reason that we should leave The Word of God and serve tables, wherefore, brethren, look ye out among you seven men of honest report, full of the Holy Ghost, and wisdom whom ye may appoint over this business. But we will give ourselves continually to prayer and the ministering of The Word." In India we have thousands of low-caste converts, very few foreign or Indian mission-

aries. It is not reason that these few should leave the
word of God and serve tables. They, as the apostles,
have had a special training for ministering The Word,
but there is this other work that must be done. It must
be done or there will be more than murmuring in the
Indian church. Let the church choose out from among
the non-theologically trained disciples, those having what
was called for in the Acts, men and women of honest report, full of the Holy Ghost, and wisdom, educators, doc-
tors, engineers, farmers, nurses, teachers of domestic
science. These are not to supplant the preacher, they are
to supplement him, to make his work more effective and
far reaching, to conserve that which the preacher began.
We frequently hear it stated that the evangelizing of the
whole world is the task of the whole church. Yet how
little provision the church has made for equipping and
sending forth any but the theologically trained. If we
call on these non-theologically trained we are widening
the scope of those actively engaged in winning the whole
world. And if we really believe that a person is better
off with Christ than without Him, we will do our utmost
to use all the gifts with which He has endowed His followers. The Apostle Paul, I. Cor. 12, speaks of the
diversity of gifts of believers, but the same Spirit controlling and directing this diversity, so that, as the result of the perfect and complete working of the various
members, we get a harmony as complete as a healthy
body where every organ is functioning properly. He
sums up with irrefutable logic, the great mystery of
our faith, ''Now ye are the body of Christ and members
in particular. And God hath set some in the church,
first apostles, secondarily prophets, thirdly teachers,
after that miracles, then gifts of healings, helps, govern-

ments, diversities of tongues." How different this teaching of Paul from some of our modern denominational papers. *God hath set in the church,* apostles, prophets, teachers, preachers, evangelists, wonderworkers, mission hospitals, leper asylums, schools and colleges. These belong in the church, are part of its God appointed equipment to carry out the greatest task in the world.

I am frequently asked if I believe the church will support such a work as I am trying to do in India, if it will not have to be separated from the church in order to grow and develop properly? I answer that all I have done has been done at the express command of duly constituted church authority, that the church at large will support such a work for it believes that God hath set in the church such things as we are trying to do for His glory.

I am told that the church should be inspirational, not institutional, that it should inspire its members to go and do outside the church what its present limitations make inconvenient to be done inside. I believe the church should be both inspirational and institutional, should have to-day as wide a program as Jesus stated and carried out and as the Apostle Paul laid down.

There are a few fundamental facts that it is well to keep in mind in a consideration of such matters as have been treated of in this book.

I. The first command God gave to man regarding the earth is "Replenish the earth, and subdue it." It is in following out this command of God to subdue the earth, to master it and make it serve mankind that man has his opportunity to develop intellect, mind and will. If man did not have this for his task, if he were like the ravens, what would he be now? It is to him that

obeys this command of God, to him that overcometh the
secrets of the natural physical world, that is given to
eat of the tree of life, which is in the midst of the para-
dise of God.   As man subdues the earth, finds out about
fire, and water, about soil and what it will do, learns the
chemical, physical, biological, economic and spiritual
laws, which He who laid the foundation of the earth
made to inhere in all matter, man not only develops
himself but with every new conquest of the laws of nature and their adaptation and appreciation, he helps to
free human life of its drudgery and monotony.   We can
see this when we compare modern transport facilities
with those of even two hundred years ago, the railroad,
steamship, motor car, airship, compared with the pack
horse and stage coach.   As labor-saving devices are
brought in the tendency in labor is from that which is
less pleasant to that which is more pleasant.   Less human physical power required, more mechanical power
and man controls by pulling levers or pressing buttons
and man multiplies his physical power **many fold.**

II. When He had finished His creation, ''God saw
everything that He had made and behold it was very
good.''   In spite of much we see about us God's world
is a good world as He created it and it is the part of
wisdom for men in general to acknowledge this.   As we
look over this world and note its constitution and order,
we notice that there are seasons, alternating periods of
rest, of rapid growth, of harvest, and then again rest.
As we think into things we must be struck with the fact
of the oft-recurring and continuing things of life;
hunger and sleep, laughter and tears, birth and growth,
and God made this world in this fashion that these
things should be so.   Therefore a great majority of the

men and women on this earth must spend their time in caring for the oft-recurring needs of men. A farmer cannot plow so that it will last for ten years. He cannot sow in one year enough wheat to last for a decade. The world is seldom ahead on its food supply more than three months. There are these daily and seasonal tasks that must be done in their appointed time. Most of them we call "secular," and there is in some theological quarters a tendency to look down upon those who do them as doing something of a lower order. I do not forget that once the heavens opened and the voice of God said of the village carpenter of Nazareth, "This is my beloved Son in whom I am well pleased." Jesus had no public ministry to His credit at that time, but it was as a carpenter that He had won this commendation from Him who rates all things at their true worth. Surely unless some farmer had saved seed and prepared his ground, sown the seed at the right time, cultivated and protected the growing crop, harvested and stored the ripened grain, which the miller took and ground and the baker took and baked into bread, the philosopher would not have his leisure to philosophize. His time for thought and study is purchased by somebody else's foresight and timely, unremitting toil. So everyone who is doing any helpful work in the world and doing it unto God, as an expression of his faith in Him who doeth all things well, who does it in faith as his share of the common task to sustain and maintain human life, need not fear in that day when all men shall be judged for what they have done. God made His world a good world, a world that gives man a chance for the fullest self-realization as he diligently obeys the commands of God with reverent spirit and

hope in his heart.   Blessed is he who does the common
task unto God.

III. In the prayer Jesus taught His disciples there is
one petition that for a long time I regarded as a lower-
ing of the standard.   On each side of it, petitions of
highest ethical and spiritual aspiration, what an appar-
ent "come down" in tone, "Give us this day our daily
bread."   How material and mundane it seems at first.
Yet let us try to leave it out and ignore what it stands
for, and see how much we lose.   Jesus was familiar with
farming operations.   He so often in his conversation
drew upon His agricultural knowledge for illustration.
So here again He talks as one having authority.   "Give
us," not me, alone, but us; the great, wide family of
mankind, Jew and Gentile, bond and free, people of
every color and tongue under heaven and all men everywhere are included in my petition.   I must think of
them when I pray.   I cannot be indifferent to the famine-
cursed anywhere on earth.   If I hear of hunger and need,
if I really pray this prayer I will do all in my power to
answer it, and help the hungry everywhere.   "Our
daily bread."   We depend daily upon God for life.   We
recognize God as the Giver of all good; but we are part-
ners with Him.   He gave the soil, the life in the seed,
the temperature, the rain, the sunshine, the increase:
man prepared the ground, plowed, and harrowed it,
sowed the seed, watched and protected it while growing,
reaped and stored the harvest against the day men
needed it.   If God had failed in any part of His share,
no harvest.   Just as true, if man fails in any part of
his, no harvest.   We are therefore co-workers together
with God.   Man is likest to God when he is doing things

to support and improve human life. So many feel that to be a Christian means to throw aside ordinary foresight and care, that somehow or other God will provide, that irresponsibility is the right attitude. This petition teaches the opposite. The bread we are to eat two years hence, where will it come from? At this very time men are exercising foresight to see that good seed is being saved in sufficient quantity, stored in proper places, protected against damp and weevil. They are plowing the ground and getting it ready for the seed. They will then throw away perfectly good seed, fit to eat, into the cold, damp ground, to run the risk of time and weather, and insect pest, and other enemies, there to die, to be lost to them, in order that there may be a harvest to provide seed for the sower and bread for the eater. As Isaiah says in this connection, "This also cometh forth from the Lord of hosts, which is wonderful in counsel and excellent in working." It is a matter of historical record that those individuals and those nations that have prayed "Give us this day our daily bread," have had this prayer more fully answered than those that have not known this prayer. There is that about the Truth that frees men. When Jesus said, "The Truth shall make you free," He was thinking in no narrow sense of truth, as being only spiritual truth. He who is The Truth, The Way, The Life, Himself The Author of all truth, is speaking of all truth, spiritual, physical, social, political, economic, in fact, any truth to which the human mind can address itself, and in subduing the earth, this great body of truth is uncovered for the blessing of men.

After Jesus had fed the multitude there remained ready for distribution if any more were needed twelve baskets of the five barley loaves. Jesus bade the disciples gather up the fragments that nothing be lost. After the years in India the greatest abiding impression that remains, is the one of "loss" in India. Appalling loss of human life, and stupendous economic waste. Human life is so abundant, so cheap, so easily given up that it is depressing. No other civilized country has such a high infant death rate. Preventable disease is ever carrying off great hosts who have survived infancy.

A man can be hired for a dollar a month. A woman or girl for less. A cooly will carry a one hundred and sixty-pound burden eight miles up a mountain side, five thousand feet high, for thirty cents. Men and women everywhere used as beasts of burden but not so well fed or housed as the beasts. The great loss due to poverty and illiteracy is beyond power to compute. India has a great religious sense, it has a great work to do. There are great isolated landmarks in Indian history where an Indian had a fair chance and where he has made use of his chance. The results are part of the precious heritage of all men everywhere. They are to be found in the various fields of knowledge, philosophy, religion, literature and science. They have enriched the world. India's future can be richer than India's past. I am always brooding over ways and means of avoiding this fearful waste of human life, of transforming it into a positive asset to enrich the world. Then there is fearful economic waste due to ignorance and superstition. If these wastes were stopped India would not be poor. The present wastes are the potential capital which should be used to get national income, the means with which to get economic independence. As Jesus looks over India to-day with its rich soil, and teeming multitudes as sheep without a shepherd, so surely does He say to those who

hear His voice, gather up the fragments that remain
that nothing of human life or of material that builds up
human life be wasted, but rather that it be conserved to
help to bless all men everywhere.   When we save India
from these incalculable losses we are helping to save one-
fifth of the human race.   A task great enough, and worth
while enough to stretch to the limit the best America has
and cause us to pray anew: The Harvest truly is plen-
teous, the laborers are few. Pray ye therefore the Lord
of the Harvest that He—God Almighty, Himself—will
send forth the laborers, men and women willing to work
out His will, properly equipped with all labor-saving devices, tractors, plows, harrows, thrashing machines, that
India may be one of the brightest jewels that ennoble
the glorious Crown of Him who once wore the Crown
of Thorns.